SUNDAY 1 SEPTEM

661 RAF fighters fly 118 patrols.   Luftwaffe effort: 530 sorties

Clear blue skies across the whole of south east England.

COMBAT A 10.45 - 11.30 hrs   Hillcoat 1 Sqn - Strasser 7/JG53

COMBAT A   10.45 – 11.30 hrs... Kent – Attack on Tilbury Docks

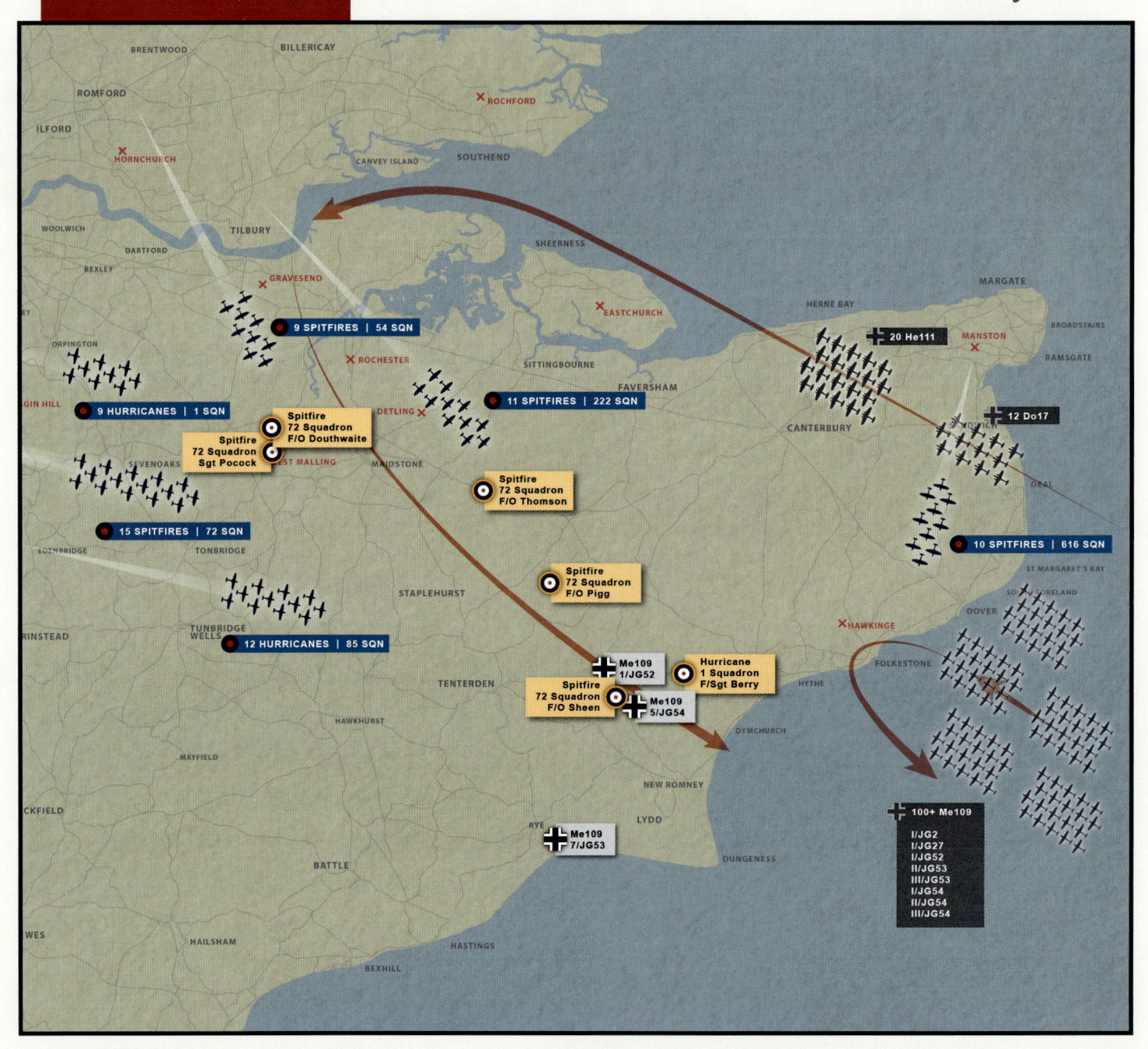

Attack on Tilbury Docks

For the past week the Luftwaffe had concentrated its attacks on Fighter Command's airfields and would continue to do so in the main. 1st September began quietly with the usual reconnaissance flights crossing the almost cloudless skies over southern England.

Plots began to appear shortly after 10.00 hours and two Spitfire squadrons, 222 and 616, were sent up to patrol the coast between Manston and Hawkinge. As predicted two formations of 50+ crossed the coast over Dover and Deal at 10.45 hours. Part of 616 Squadron engaged over Dover and were prevented from reaching the bombers by the Me109s, but the Spitfire pilots believed that the bombers then turned back.

The second raid made its way across Kent to the Thames Estuary and turned west. The RAF believed the intended target to be Hornchurch airfield, but Luftwaffe records show that Tilbury Docks were the real target for just twelve bombers with a huge fighter escort. Only 222 Squadron engaged prior to the bombing and scattered bombs fell in the Tilbury/Thames area. The force withdrew over Kent harried by 1, 54, 72 and 85 Squadrons.

RAF Victory Claims

1 September 1940 - 10.45 - 11.30 hrs Combat A. attack on Tilbury Docks.

RAF Victory Claims		Combat A	10.45 – 11.30 hrs
616 Sqn	P/O J Brewster	Me109 destroyed	off Folkestone
616 Sqn	F/Lt D E Gillam	Me109 probable	Folkestone - Dungeness
616 Sqn	P/O L H Casson	Me109 probable	Dungeness - Mid Channel
616 Sqn	F/Sgt Bernard	Me109 probable	Folkestone - Dungeness
616 Sqn	S/Ldr M Robinson	Me109 damaged	Folkestone - Dungeness
616 Sqn	P/O J Brewster	Me109 damaged	off Folkestone
616 Sqn	P/O J Brewster	Me109 damaged	off Folkestone
616 Sqn	P/O K Holden	Me109 damaged	Folkestone
616 Sqn	P/O K Holden	Me109 damaged	Folkestone
616 Sqn	F/Sgt Bernard	Me109 damaged	Folkestone - Dungeness
222 Sqn	S/Ldr J H Hill	Me109 probable	Canterbury
222 Sqn	P/O T A Vigors	Me109 probable	Canterbury
222 Sqn	P/O J M V Carpenter	Me109 probable	Canterbury
1 Sqn	P/O P V Boot	Me109 destroyed	off the French Coast
1 Sqn	F/Lt H B L Hillcoat	Me109 destroyed	east of Tunbridge
1 Sqn	P/O C N Birch	Me109 destroyed	Tonbridge to Gravesend
1 Sqn	P/O C A C Chetham	Me109 destroyed	Tonbridge to Gravesend
54 Sqn	P/O C F Gray	He111 destroyed	Maidstone
72 Sqn	P/O B Douthwaite	Me109 destroyed	Gatwick to Rye
72 Sqn	P/O D C Winter	He113 destroyed	north of Beachy Head
72 Sqn	F/O J W Villa	Me109 damaged	Gatwick
72 Sqn	Sgt M Gray	Do17 probable	2 miles west of Rye
85 Sqn	P/O G Allard	Me109 destroyed	Dover
85 Sqn	Sgt G Goodman	Me109 destroyed	Dover

F/Lt D E Gillam 616 Sqn

S/Ldr M Robinson 616 Sqn

F/Lt H B L Hillcoat 1 Sqn

P/O L H Casson 616 Sqn

Luftwaffe Victory Claims

1 September 1940 - 10.45 - 11.30 hrs Combat A. attack on Tilbury Docks.

Luftwaffe Victory Claims		Combat A	10.45 – 11.30 hrs
1/JG2	Fw Erich Rudorffer	Spitfire	Dover
2/JG27	Fw Willi Kothmann	Curtiss	London
Stab I/JG52	Lt Hans Berthel	Hurricane	Sittingbourne
1/JG52	Lt Franz Essl	Spitfire	south east of Ashford
1/JG52	Fw Heinz Uerlings	Spitfire	Ashford-Folkestone
2/JG52	Oblt Helmut Bennemann	Spitfire	Sittingbourne
2/JG52	Oblt Karl-Heinz Leesmann	Spitfire	Sittingbourne
Stab II/JG53	Hptm Günther Frhr v Maltzahn	Spitfire	
Stab III/JG53	Hptm Wolf-Dietrich Wilcke	Spitfire	
7/JG53	Uffz Adolf Kalkum	Hurricane	Thames Estuary
7/JG53	Uffz Hans-Georg Schulte	Hurricane	Thames Estuary
7/JG53	Fw Werner Stumpf	Hurricane	Thames Estuary
3/JG54	Oblt Adolf-Waldemar Kinzinger	Spitfire	Tenterden
4/JG54	Oblt Hans Philipp	Spitfire u/c	Thames Estuary
Stab III/JG54	Lt Hans-Erich Heinbockel	Spitfire	6km east of Ashford

COMBAT B

13.30 to 14.45 hrs... Kent
Attacks on Biggin Hill and Kenley

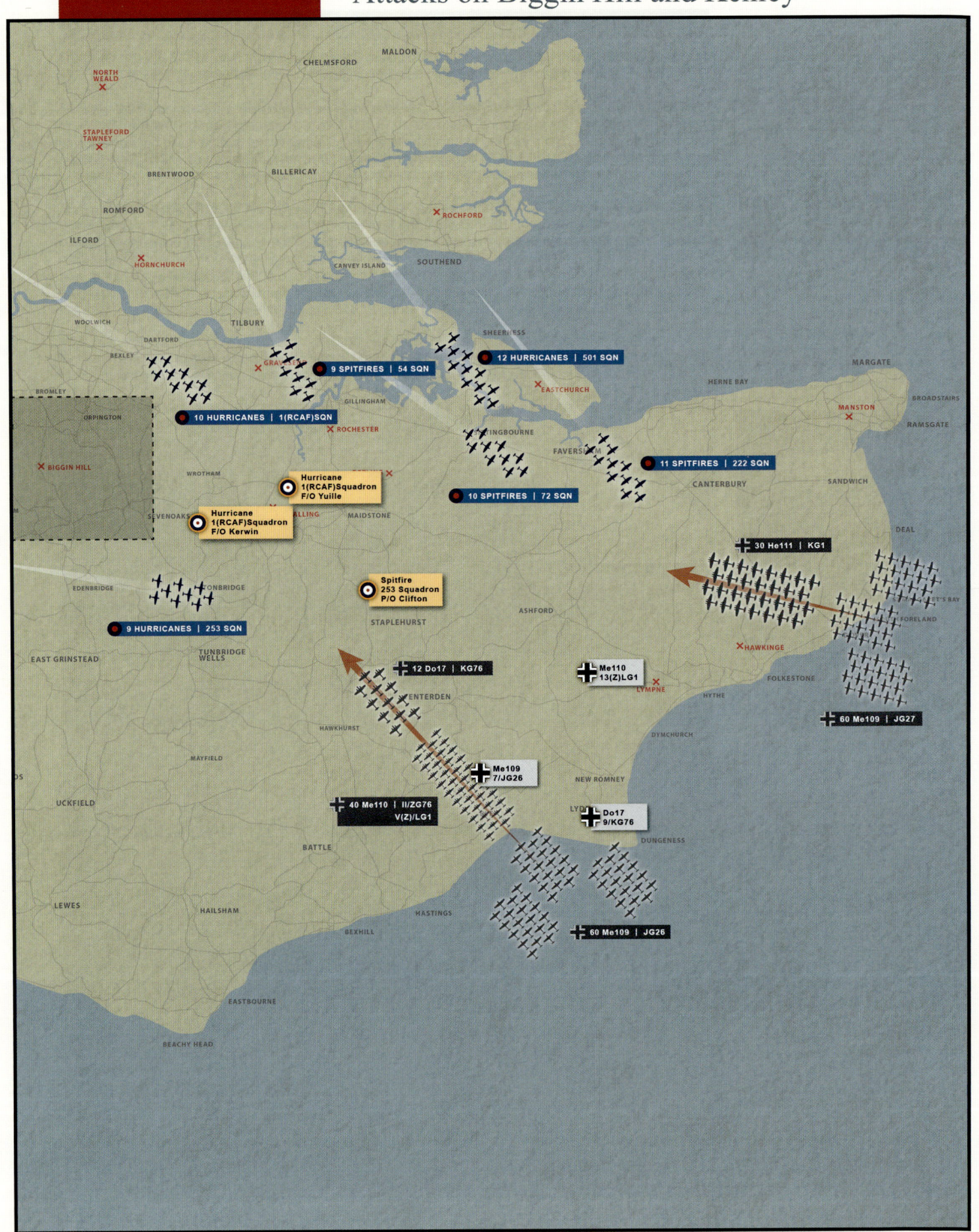

The Attacks on Biggin Hill and Kenley
1 September 1940 - 13.30 - 14.45 hrs Combat B. Kent

Spitfires of 72 and 222 Squadrons had been scrambled to patrol eastern Kent to look out for reconnaissance aircraft when two raids were plotted crossing the Dover Straits at 13.30 hours. Three further squadrons were then scrambled:

253 Squadron – 9 Hurricanes up from Kenley to patrol Dungeness.
54 Squadron – 9 Spitfires up from Hornchurch to patrol Canterbury.
85 Squadron – 11 Hurricanes up from Croydon to patrol Tunbridge Wells.

The pilots of 72 Squadron encountered '40 Do17 and He111s, with rather more Me109s and Me110s' not the 12+ they had been expecting, as the enemy crossed the coast at Dungeness heading towards Tunbridge Wells and then Biggin Hill. These were the Do17s of KG76 escorted by Me110s of II/ZG76 and V(Z)/LG1 with Me109s of JG26. A further five squadrons were then scrambled:

1 (RCAF) Squadron – 10 Hurricanes up from Northolt to intercept raiders near Biggin Hill.
79 Squadron – 12 Hurricanes up from Biggin Hill to patrol base.
616 Squadron – 5 Spitfires up from Kenley to patrol base.
303 Squadron – 12 Hurricanes up from Northolt to patrol base.
501 Squadron – 12 Hurricanes up from Gravesend to patrol Maidstone.

Ten squadrons were airborne when Biggin Hill and the surrounding area was bombed at 14.00 hours, but none of the defending fighters engaged until the bombers were withdrawing. The Hurricanes of 85 and 79 Squadrons were 'bounced' by Me109s whilst climbing to meet the raid and a running fight ensued across Kent to the coast. This was the fourth major attack suffered by Biggin Hill and many buildings not already ruined were significantly weakened and in danger of collapse.

The second raid had by this time crossed the coast over Hythe and was estimated at 100+. Nine Hurricanes of 253 Squadron dived out of the sun onto the '50 bombers and 100 fighters' The pilots claimed to have broken up the formation and, indeed, bombers were widely scattered over central Kent without there being any obvious target.

The Luftwaffe over estimated its success, but Fighter Command over estimated the number of bombers involved – possibly identifying the Me110 escort as 'bombers':

14.00 hrs Kenley. 12 aircraft bombed - hits on hangars, airfield and buildings.
14.00 hrs Biggin Hill. 3 aircraft bombed - hits on two hangars, airfield and barracks.
14.05 hrs Abingdon. 2 aircraft bombed - hits on hangars, airfield and buildings.
15.35 hrs Hawkinge. 8 SC250s dropped on the airfield.
15.35 hrs Lympne. 4 SC250s dropped on the airfield. 2 or 3 aircraft destroyed.
16.40 hrs Detling. 6 SC250s dropped on the airfield. 3 aircraft destroyed.

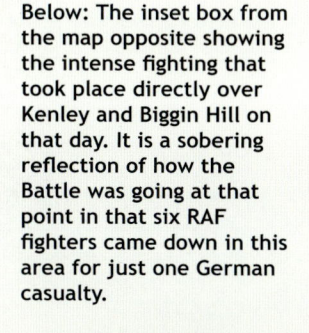

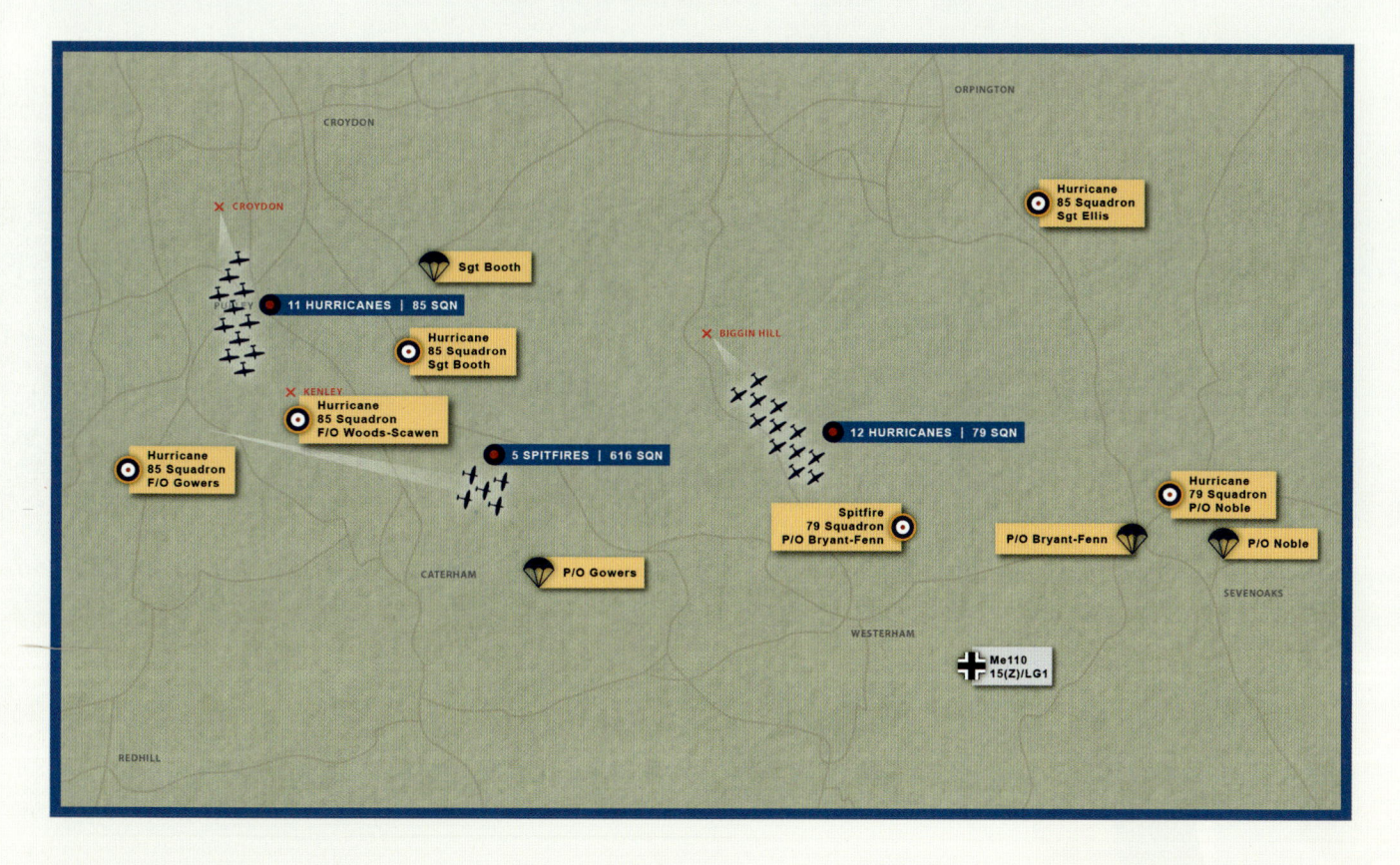

Below: The inset box from the map opposite showing the intense fighting that took place directly over Kenley and Biggin Hill on that day. It is a sobering reflection of how the Battle was going at that point in that six RAF fighters came down in this area for just one German casualty.

Contemporary Accounts 79 Sqn

1 September 1940 - 13.30 - 14.45 hrs Combat B. Kent

79 SQUADRON OPERATIONS RECORD BOOK

At about 14.00 hours eleven aircraft took off. Twenty bombers and about 100 enemy fighters seen. F/Lt Haysom crashed on drome on landing, he claims 1 Do 215 damaged. P/O Stones, DFC 1 Do 17 or 215 probable. P/O Peters 1 Do 17 probable. P/O Mayhew 1 Do 17 destroyed. P/O Clift 1 Me 110 probable. P/O Bryant-Fenn and P/O Noble missing, later learned to be in hospital wounded. Remainder landed at 15.00 hours.

COMBAT REPORT:
F/Lt Haysom – B Flight, 79 Squadron

Patrolled base 12 – 15,000 feet before reaching this height wave of bombers passed over from west to east about 4,000 feet above. Bombs dropped west of base. E/a travelled east to Ashford turned round and did another cut on base. Attempted quarter attack on extreme e/a (bomber) broke off attack owing to attack by 110. Evaded e/a. Bomber formation turned south almost devoid of fighter escort – attacked e/a on extreme right – fired one long burst from dead astern – no return fire observed – attacked from rear by 109 – broke off attack – result of fire not observed. U/C collapsed on landing. A/C shot up from rear.

COMBAT REPORT:
P/O D W A Stones – A Flight, 79 Squadron

I took off as an individual member of 'A' Flight on aerodrome defence at 14.08 hours 1.9.40. Climbed to 15,000 feet and intercepted 20 Do17s and an escort of approximately 100 Messerschmitts 109 and 110. I attacked the rearmost Do17 and started firing at 250 yards – overtaking speed was only about 15 – 20 m.p.h. I put a long burst into him from dead astern and gradually closed to about 50 yards where I finished my rounds. I saw my fire enter his port engine and part of his port wing. I broke away without observing any result, and dog fought a Me110, having no ammunition. Landed 14.30.

Note. A great deal of German talking heard over the R/T.

COMBAT REPORT:
P/O Mayhew – B Flight, 79 Squadron

At 13.15 hours B Flight of 79 Squadron was ordered to scramble and patrol base on Station Defence. A large force of bombers was sighted, but I was unable to reach their height. When I had climbed to 15,000 feet I saw about 12 Dorniers, escorted by an equal number of fighters Me109s over Westerham flying north-west. The fighters appeared to be already engaged, so I attacked the bomber formation from in front and to the left. No.3 of the leading vic turned head on to me. As we passed I turned sharply and came on its tail. Attacked from astern by unknown fighter, but succeeded in shaking him off. Returned to port quarter attack, and opened fire at 230 yards, holding an 8 seconds burst until it developed to a stern chase which I broke off at a range of 75 yards. I saw tracer entering cockpit and engines. The port engine let out smoke machine soared up, stalled and went into a quick spin. I followed down and saw it crash in the corner of a wood two miles south-east of Westerham. It exploded violently and burnt out.

Contemporary Accounts 72 Sqn

1 September 1940 - 13.30 - 14.45 hrs Combat B. Kent

72 SQUADRON OPERATIONS RECORD BOOK

12.50 hrs. 10 Spitfires took off from Croydon to patrol Hawkinge at 15,000 feet. A large formation of bombers was intercepted near Dungeness, escorted by Me109s and Me110s. 10 Spitfires landed Croydon 14.20 hours.

COMBAT REPORT:
F/Lt E Graham - Tennis Leader - Blue 1, B Flight, 72 Squadron

At 13.15 hours the squadron consisting of a Blue leading section of 3 a/c, a Red section of 3 a/c and a rearguard of 4 a/c encountered about 30 or 40 Do17s (presumed) approaching the coast at 15,000 feet. I decided to attack from head-on, but had to break off the attack before it had been delivered on account of 40 or 50 Me109s diving down from about 20,000 feet on to our tails. These Me109s had been flying ahead of the Do17s and it was a simple matter for them to foil our initial head-on attack. I was forced to fight the Me109s and in the ensuing dog fight damaged two Me109s. In a very short space of time I was out of ammunition and was fortunate in gaining cover in thin cloud at 14,000 ft. I managed to return to base and on landing my aircraft was found to have 3 bullets in the oil tank. Aircraft put unserviceable.

COMBAT REPORT:
P/O T A F Elsdon - B Flight, 72 Squadron

When I first saw the formation of about 20 Me Jaguar or Me110s they were flying in two Vics north east. At the same time I saw two Me109s in my rear-view mirror. Whilst evading these I became separated from my section and the Me109s dived away. As I approached the Me Jaguars they formed a circle in tight line astern. I attacked from slightly above and towards the centre of the circle gradually decreasing the deflection to about 30°. Range about 400 – 200 yds. This produced no result except that the aircraft closed up in line astern.

In my second attack I decided to keep a steady burst into the circle and let them fly through. I finished my rounds in this manner and during one burst two of them went down. An eye-witness (Sgt Rolls) on the ground saw the machines falling and crash into the ground and confirmed that they were from a circle of aircraft very high up and to the south east of Croydon.

Apart from the two Me109s in the first instance no other fighters were encountered.

No other pilot reported seeing bombers form a circle as an evasion tactic.

COMBAT REPORT:
P/O D F Holland - Red 3, A Flight, 72 Squadron

I was flying in Red 3. We had been told to look out for E/A when an Me109 made an attack on me from above. I did not see him until he started firing, when I could see his tracer bullets passing over my port wing. I then did a steep turn to the left and got on his tail. I gave him a burst of about 2 seconds when I was attacked by 3 or more Me109s firing at me in all directions. To get away I did a flick half roll to the left and dived down to a height of 2,000 ft. I then joined with Red 1 again and returned to base. I have no idea what happened to the Me109 I attacked.

Contemporary Accounts 54 & 501 Sqns

1 September 1940 - 13.30 - 14.45 hrs Combat B. Kent

54 SQUADRON INTELLIGENCE REPORT

Nine Spitfires of 54 Squadron left Hornchurch at 13.30 hours to patrol Canterbury at 20,000 feet. They were later vectored to Biggin Hill to intercept enemy bombers which they sighted at 14.15 hours at 20,000 feet with an escort of about forty Me109s above with yellow noses. There were about 20 bombers in all, consisting of Do17s or 215s and Me110s. The Me110s formed a defensive circle when seen. The under surfaces of the Me109s were coloured light blue and in some cases light silver. Seven Spitfires landed Rochford at 14.50 hours and two at Hornchurch at 14.45 hours.

> *I pulled up from the bombers to 28,000 feet, and I saw an Me109 only 50 yards away below to the left. I turned over on my back and, with a steep dive turn fired through the roof of e/a as I turned. E/A dropped and I think the pilot was hit. This Me109 had yellow wing tips.*
> P/O S Baker - Green 2, B Flight, 54 Squadron

COMBAT REPORT:
P/O C F Gray - Green 1, B Flight, 54 Squadron

I was 25,000 feet over Biggin Hill with Green Section when I sighted enemy bombers escorted by Me109s and Me110s. The bombers were in Vics of three in parallel lines. I shot down an Me109, and saw Glycol fumes and then the engine stopped. I followed E/A down 10,000 feet. The pilot was looking for a place to land. E/A was uniformly coloured silvery blue.

Above: Colin Gray's victim was a 7/JG26 Me109 like this one, flown by Josef Bürschgens (pictured left). This Gruppe retained very pale blue polished fuselage sides to their 109s which perfectly match Gray's description of a silvery blue colour. Note also the yellow wingtips as described by Stanley Baker in his combat report extract above.

501 SQUADRON INTELLIGENCE REPORT

12 Hurricanes of No.501 Squadron left Gravesend at 14.10 hours. They were 'vectored' south-east towards Maidstone at 15,000 feet, and encountered, coming towards them at 16,000 feet a force of 27 Me 110s. They climbed and circled round to attack the Me 110s in the rear, but the latter turned the movement, and did a 'beam' attack upon them. Only one section was engaged, and Yellow 2 was able to damage one of the Me 110s. Before they approached the Me 110s, they had seen them engaged with other Hurricanes and Spitfires. No enemy bombers were seen on this occasion. 12 Hurricanes returned to Gravesend by 15.10 hours.

Contemporary Accounts 253 Sqn
1 September 1940 - 13.30 - 14.45 hrs Combat B. Kent

253 SQUADRON INTELLIGENCE REPORT

9 Hurricanes took off Kenley 13.30 hours. Several orders were given and finally Hurricanes were vectored 120 degrees Dungeness area. 150 enemy aircraft comprising of some 50 Do 215s and He111s escorted by 100 Me 110s and Me109s and possibly He113s, were sighted stepped up between 15,000 and 22,000 feet. The squadron went into sections of shallow echelons, turned to port and dived onto the main bomber formation out of the sun, spraying them with incendiary. This attack considered by all pilots taking part most successful although no results observed as enemy fighters were closing in. The squadron formation then broke up and pilots harried the enemy inland and back to the coast.

A peculiarity was that pilots saw Me109s below bombers and fighters above.

Red 1 (F/Lt Wedgewood) fired 3 two second bursts into Do 215 silencing rear gunner and then later attacked a bomber (type uncertain) and observed small pieces breaking away.

Red 3 (P/O Greenwood) in a dive out of sun into Do 215s fired a 6 second burst observing a cloud of black smoke emitting from e/a and a glow.

8 aircraft landed Kenley 14.30 hours.
Our casualties.					1 Hurricane lost.- P/O Clifton killed.

COMBAT REPORT:
F/Lt W P Cambridge - Blue 1, B Flight, 253 Squadron

I was leading 253 Squadron as Blue One when near the coast we observed a very large enemy formation. I brought the squadron into line abreast with sections in shallow echelon and from a height of 20,000 feet dived out of the sun onto the bombers which were 5,000 feet below. No results were observed as the enemy fighters were now on our tails. I lost the formation and received instructions from controller to return to base which was then being bombed. I gained height and tried to carry out attack on enemy bombers but was intercepted by Me 110s which I evaded by darting into clouds. I then climbed to 22,000 feet. I saw enemy formation was heading east and approached one which had fallen slightly behind main formation of Me 110s. I got on top and dived out of sun. I opened fire rather early and noticed bullets were falling short. I corrected for this and when I was within about 400 yards noticed rear gunner was firing at me. He was soon silenced and I closed to point blank range firing steadily. The other Me110s had meanwhile started forming a circle and I did not wait to see the result.

Below: Photos of 253 Squadron Hurricanes in the Battle of Britain are very rare, this one was taken in spring 1940 at Northolt showing an SW coded 253 Hurricane being refuelled. Note the external armoured windscreen which had been replaced by an internal version on most Hurricanes by the start of the Battle.

RAF Casualties continued

1 September 1940 - 13.30 - 14.45 hrs Combat B. Kent

| RAF Casualties continued | Combat B | 13.30 to 14.45 hrs |

85 Sqn Hurricane P3150 VY-Z F/O P P Woods-Scawen – killed. Shot down by Me109s during combat over Kenley and fell into a garden between Welcomes Road and Hermitage Road, Kenley. Pilot baled out but killed due to parachute failure. Body found on 6.9.40 in the grounds of The Ivies, Kenley Lane.

85 Sqn Hurricane N2477 VY-L P/O G Allard – safe. Forced-landed at Lympne due to loss of oil pressure then caught in bombing attack. Aircraft damaged.

85 Sqn Hurricane L2071 VY-O Sgt G B Booth – wounded. Shot down by Me109s and crashed into Kingswood, Sanderstead, Surrey. Pilot baled out with burns and parachute alight. Further injured in a heavy landing at 115 Littleheath Road, Selsdon, and admitted to Purley Hospital. Died on 7th February 1941 in Horton Hospital, Epsom, Surrey.

85 Sqn Hurricane P2673 VY-E Sgt J H M Ellis – missing. Failed to return following combat with Me109s over Kenley area. Ellis remained 'missing' until 1993 when human remains found in a Hurricane wreck at Chelsfield were identified as his.

85 Sqn Hurricane P3151 VY-Y P/O A G Lewis – safe. Landed at base with undercarriage up following combat with Me109s over Kenley. An enquiry put this down to 'pilot error' as he forgot to lower it.

253 Sqn Hurricane P5185 P/O J K G Clifton – killed. Shot down in combat with Do 215s and Bf 110s over Dungeness. Crashed at Clapper Lane, Staplehurst.

616 Sqn Spitfire R6778 P/O L H Casson – safe. Hit in port wing and oil tank by cannon fire during attack on a Do17 over Kenley. Aircraft was landed safely but was subsequently written-off.

Patrick Philip Woods-Scawen DFC (24)
Born: Karachi, India.
Joined the RAF in 1937.
Joined 85 Sqn in August 1938.
Combat claims - 17
9 in the Battle of France.
29/7/40 Do17 damaged.
26/8/40 Me109 probable.
26/8/40 Do17 shared.
28/8/40 Me109 destroyed.
30/8/40 Me110 destroyed.
31/8/40 Me109 destroyed.
31/8/40 Me109 destroyed.
31/8/40 Me109 destroyed.

John Kenneth Grahame Clifton (21)
Born: Plymouth.
Joined the RAF in 1939.
Joined 253 Sqn in November 1939.
Combat claims - 3
18/5/40 Do17 destroyed.
19/5/40 Me109 probable.
31/8/40 He111 destroyed.

Glendon Bulmar Booth (19)
Born: Sydenham, Kent.
Joined the RAF in 1939.
Joined 85 Sqn on 15th July 1940.
Combat claims - 3
29/8/40 Me109 damaged.
30/8/40 Me110 damaged.
31/8/40 Me110 probable.

John Hugh Mortimer Ellis (21)
Born: Cambridge.
Joined the RAF in 1938.
Joined 85 Sqn in May 1940.
Combat claims - 3
6/8/40 Me109 destroyed.
18/8/40 Me110 damaged.
26/8/40 Do17 destroyed.

The Strange Case of John 'Hugh' Ellis
1 September 1940 - 13.30 - 14.45 hrs Combat B. Kent

At 13.50 hours 85 Squadron was scrambled from Croydon to intercept a raid, estimated to be between 150 and 200 aircraft, as it approached Biggin Hill. As the Hurricanes climbed over Kenley they were 'bounced' by a group of Me109s. The Hurricane pilots of 79 Squadron had similarly been scrambled from Biggin Hill and, as they also climbed to meet the raid, they too were 'bounced'. The Me109s from JG26, including 'Aces' like Galland and Schöpfel, came from above and passed through the Hurricanes which were 'cut to pieces'. Within minutes six Hurricanes were falling from the sky.

Trevor Bryant-Fenn and Brian Noble described their experiences to historian Colin Brown in 1984.

'Biggin Hill was under regular air attack at the time so pilots were dispersed at night. I and two others spent the Saturday night at the home of Sir Waldron Smithers MP at Knockholt. I well recall chatting with Sir Waldron and Lady Smithers in their garden after breakfast before returning to the airfield. It was a beautiful sunny morning, not a cloud in sight.

'There had been a lot of activity already on Sunday 1st September and the readiness aircraft were airborne. At about mid-day an order came through to scramble all available aircraft to patrol over Biggin at 20,000 feet. There were only two aircraft, mine W6670 and the other flown by Brian Noble. We took off and gained height and at about 17,000 feet saw a mass of aircraft with fighter cover above us and heading for London. We climbed to their height and identified about 30 Dornier 17s with Me109s behind and above. Brian Noble was echelon starboard to me. I got a Dornier in my sights and pressed the firing button when tracer fire started overtaking me from behind. I felt a thump on the leg and a fire started down by the right rudder pedal. Flames started building up in the cockpit so I decided to quit. The next thing I remember is being on the end of a parachute – some Me109s milling around and another parachute not far away.

'A Hurricane was in a vertical dive in flames – probably mine. I landed at Dunton Green. I am not sure where my aircraft ended up. The other parachute had Brian Noble on the end – he landed in the Marley lake at Riverhead. We met again some hours later in the same ward at Sevenoaks Hospital.'

Trevor Bryant-Fenn

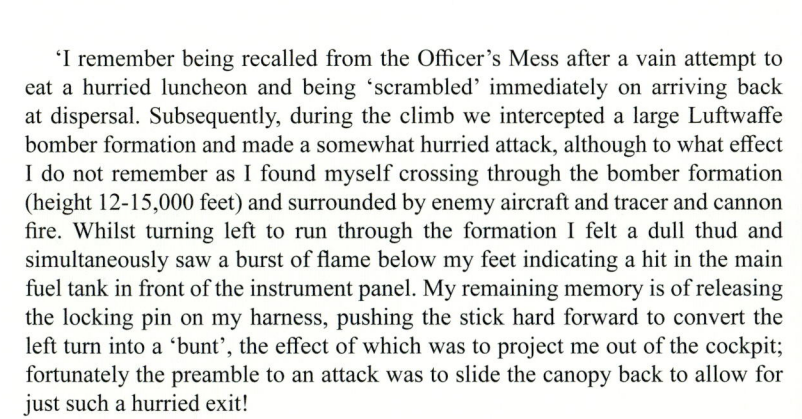

'I remember being recalled from the Officer's Mess after a vain attempt to eat a hurried luncheon and being 'scrambled' immediately on arriving back at dispersal. Subsequently, during the climb we intercepted a large Luftwaffe bomber formation and made a somewhat hurried attack, although to what effect I do not remember as I found myself crossing through the bomber formation (height 12-15,000 feet) and surrounded by enemy aircraft and tracer and cannon fire. Whilst turning left to run through the formation I felt a dull thud and simultaneously saw a burst of flame below my feet indicating a hit in the main fuel tank in front of the instrument panel. My remaining memory is of releasing the locking pin on my harness, pushing the stick hard forward to convert the left turn into a 'bunt', the effect of which was to project me out of the cockpit; fortunately the preamble to an attack was to slide the canopy back to allow for just such a hurried exit!

I recall having some trouble pulling the parachute ripcord – my hands having been burned – and I lost some nails on both hands. I recall only two brief moments whilst parachuting down – one of being close to another parachuting airman at one time, whilst both of us were 'investigated' by a friendly fighter and secondly of being over water into which I fell almost immediately. This in fact was the Marley sand and gravel pit at Riverhead, Sevenoaks and from which I was promptly rescued by the local LDV, one of whom took me to the local hospital at Sevenoaks, where I was to spend the next month in company with Trevor Bryant-Fenn, my section leader on that sortie.'

Brian Noble

The Strange Case of John 'Hugh' Ellis
1 September 1940 - 13.30 - 14.45 hrs Combat B. Kent

Patrick Woods-Scawen, was leading five Hurricanes of 85 Squadron's 'B' Flight when it was 'bounced'. His Hurricane was seen to spiral down and crash in a meadow between Welcomes Road and Hermitage Road, not far from Kenley airfield. Police and ARP reported the crash and the local fire brigade put out the burning grass, but there was no sign of the pilot's body. It was hoped that he had managed to bale out and that he would appear again in the mess that evening, but he did not. His body was found five days later in thick undergrowth at a house called 'The Ivies' in Kenley Lane. His parachute was unopened.

Arthur Gowers' Hurricane was set on fire just south of Kenley. He baled out with serious burns. 19-year-old Glendon Booth's Hurricane was also set alight. He baled out from his blazing cockpit but his clothing and parachute were both on fire. Witnesses looked on as Glendon, with one shoe on and one off, his clothing tattered and flapping behind him, collided with a telephone pole and then fell onto a rose arch. A cannon shell had hit his parachute pack, damaging it so that the canopy failed to deploy correctly, his high-speed landing had broken a leg, and arm, and fractured his spine. Paralysed by his spinal injury he fought for life until succumbing to a kidney infection five months later.

Three of 'B' Flight's five pilots had been shot down within minutes.

Of the fourth member of 85 Squadron, from 'A' Flight, 21-year-old John Ellis, there was no news.

Over the following hours, five of the six aircraft wrecks were located and reports written. 79 Squadron reported at 23.10 hours that night that Hurricane L2062 had been shot down over Chelsfield and that its pilot, Brian Noble, was in Sevenoaks Hospital. Salvage was required. The missing aircraft was that of 'Hugh' Ellis - he was reported as 'missing', and his parents duly informed.

On September 13th John Ellis's father wrote to the Air Ministry:

September 13th 1940

Dear Sir,

Reference C7/742068

I duly received your letter of September 3rd confirming your wire of a day or two previously that my son Sergt John Hugh Mortimer Ellis of No.85 Squadron R.A.F. is missing.
I rather expected that something more would have been discovered by this time as I understand the action from which he failed to return was over the Kenley area of Surrey on Sunday afternoon, September 1st.
I take it a machine and pilot could not remain undiscovered coming down on the land in the middle of the day for any length of time. I also trust that all possible measures are taken to trace missing and so allay the terrible suspense of waiting for news.
My son was very keen on doing all he possibly could for the 'Air Force' and his country. I should like to feel that the 'Air Force' are as keen on investigating all avenues that might throw light on his absence.
I would very much like to know if any of his colleagues who took part in this action could throw any light on the matter, or if you have any suggestions to advance.
One feels so helpless to do anything and would like to feel reassured that everything possible is being done to find out what has happened.
Please let me have an early reply and oblige.

I am,
Yours sincerely
F J Ellis

There being no urgency, three weeks passed before a firm of civilian contractors arrived at Chelsfield to recover the wreckage of the Hurricane that Brian Noble had baled out from. The contractors, A V Nichols, reported to the RAF's 49 Maintenance Unit on September 24th that during their recovery they had found a flying boot with a foot inside, a parachute and finally the 'Pilot's body'. The 'body' with its personal effects were handed to the police, the hole was filled in and the workers went on to their next job.

The news that a body had been recovered from the Chelsfield crash site, which of course should have contained no body or parachute, went unnoticed by 49 Maintenance Unit and no other office of the Air Ministry was informed. The 'body', now in the hands of the Police, was not identified and no written record was kept of its fate.

The Strange Case of John 'Hugh' Ellis
1 September 1940 - 13.30 - 14.45 hrs Combat B. Kent

Enquiries continued and Squadron Leader Peter Townsend, Commanding Office of 85 Squadron, replied to the Air Ministry on 4th October 1940 stating *"It is presumed that Sergeant Ellis was shot down by enemy fighters before having time to engage the bombers, and that he crashed in the Biggin Hill – Kenley area. Search for his body and aircraft was undertaken by Kenley, but up till now no word has been received from them."*

There being no further information regarding John Ellis, his father was informed that death was now to be presumed, as was standard procedure for an airman lost at sea. His father still questioned how his son could simply disappear when so far from the sea:

Dear Sir,

28th February 1941.

I duly received yours of the 26th inst, and note that as no news has been received of my son J H M Ellis, it is proposed to take official action to presume his death.
I very much regret to say that I have heard nothing further respecting my son, or have any evidence regarding him at all.
I should very much like to know if the absence of any news means that you have found no trace of his 'Hurricane', which should be possible to identify by Registration No. or something, or if he has simply vanished without a trace of either himself or his plane.
I am naturally anxious to know if possible what has happened to him, even if the news is not pleasant. Thanking you in anticipation of your early reply,

I am
Yours faithfully,
F J Ellis

The Air Commodore in charge of records took up the father's case: He wrote to Peter Townsend,
"It is felt that it is hardly conceivable that no trace of aircraft or airman should have been found in the area referred to during a period of six months and that the next of kin may very well feel this too. I am therefore referring the matter to you with the request that you will communicate with Mr Ellis in due course."

Peter Townsend, now a Wing Commander, finalised the matter with a further letter to Hugh's father that came to the conclusion that he had indeed been lost to the sea and that his body would never be found:

Reference No: No.85 Squadron,
858/701/13/P.1 R.A.F. Station,
Debden, Essex

4th April, 1941.

Dear Mr Ellis,

I have with me a copy of a letter from you to the Air Officer i/c Records, requesting news of your son Hugh. We have had to reply to the Air Ministry and inform them that we have received no further news of your son's death. We suspected, you remember, that he lost his life in the neighbourhood of Kenley, but as neither that Station nor any other can produce evidence of his having been killed in their sectors, we are now forced to the conclusion that he was killed over the sea. This conclusion is supported by the fact that F/Lt Allard his section leader, made a forced landing at Lympne and had presumably been engaged over the sea or near the coast.

Yours sincerely,
(sgd) P W Townsend,
Wing Commander, Commanding,
No.85 Squadron, R.A.F.

Other Luftwaffe Casualties

1 September 1940

Other Luftwaffe Casualties

5/JG27 Me109E-4 Wn.1420 10% damaged in combat, landed near Douvres. Ff: Oblt Emmerich Fluder - safe.

4/JG54 Me109E-4 Damaged by fighters and landed in the sea. Ff: Ofw Paul Hier safe - rescued by Seenotdienst. Or states damaged by own Flak, force-landed (Prien).

7/JG54 Me109E-3 Wn.1647 White 11 10% damaged in combat, landed at St Inglevert. Ff: Lt Max-Hellmuth Ostermann safe.

14(Z)/LG1 Me110C-4 Wn.3544 L1+DK 50% damaged by fighters over London. Crew safe.

6/ZG76 Me110C-4 Wn.3071 2N+EM Landed due to damage by fighters at Laval 50%. Crew safe.

1/KGr100 He111H-3 Wn.5687 6N+OH Landed at St Brieuc due to fuel shortage following raid on Liverpool. Crew safe. 30% damage.

2/KGr100 He111H-1 Wn.5100 6N+MK Crashed on landing at Vannes following raid on Liverpool. Crew safe. 60% damage.

1(F)/22 Me110C-5 Wn.2206 4N+CH Crashed on landing at Ostende following reconnaissance sortie. Crew safe. 40% damage.

Night Operations

1/2 September 1940

Below: A Heinkel 111 heads for England at dusk.

Luftflotte 3 carried out an attack on Swansea by 13 Ju88s of LG1, 34 He111s of KG27, 8 Ju88s of KGr806, 14 Do17s of KGr606, 1 He111 of StG3 and 1 He111 of KGr100. One Ju88 crashed on return.

Luftwaffe Casualty — Night 1st - 2nd

7/LG1 Ju88A-1 Wn.7009 L1+FR Crashed on landing at Châteaudun 100%. Ff: Oblt Helmut Hirsch and Bf: Ogefr Heinz Richter both killed. Bo: Uffz Günther Sirlin and Bs: Gefr Erich Beck both badly wounded.

MONDAY 2 SEPTEMBER

741 RAF fighters fly 100 patrols.   Luftwaffe effort: 100 bomber - 872 fighter sorties

Fog and mist in the early morning, then a fine warm day in south east England.

COMBAT C 16.30 - 17.15hrs Parnall 249 Sqn - Wrede 4/ZG76

COMBAT A

07.45 - 08.15 hrs... Kent
Attack on Gravesend Docks

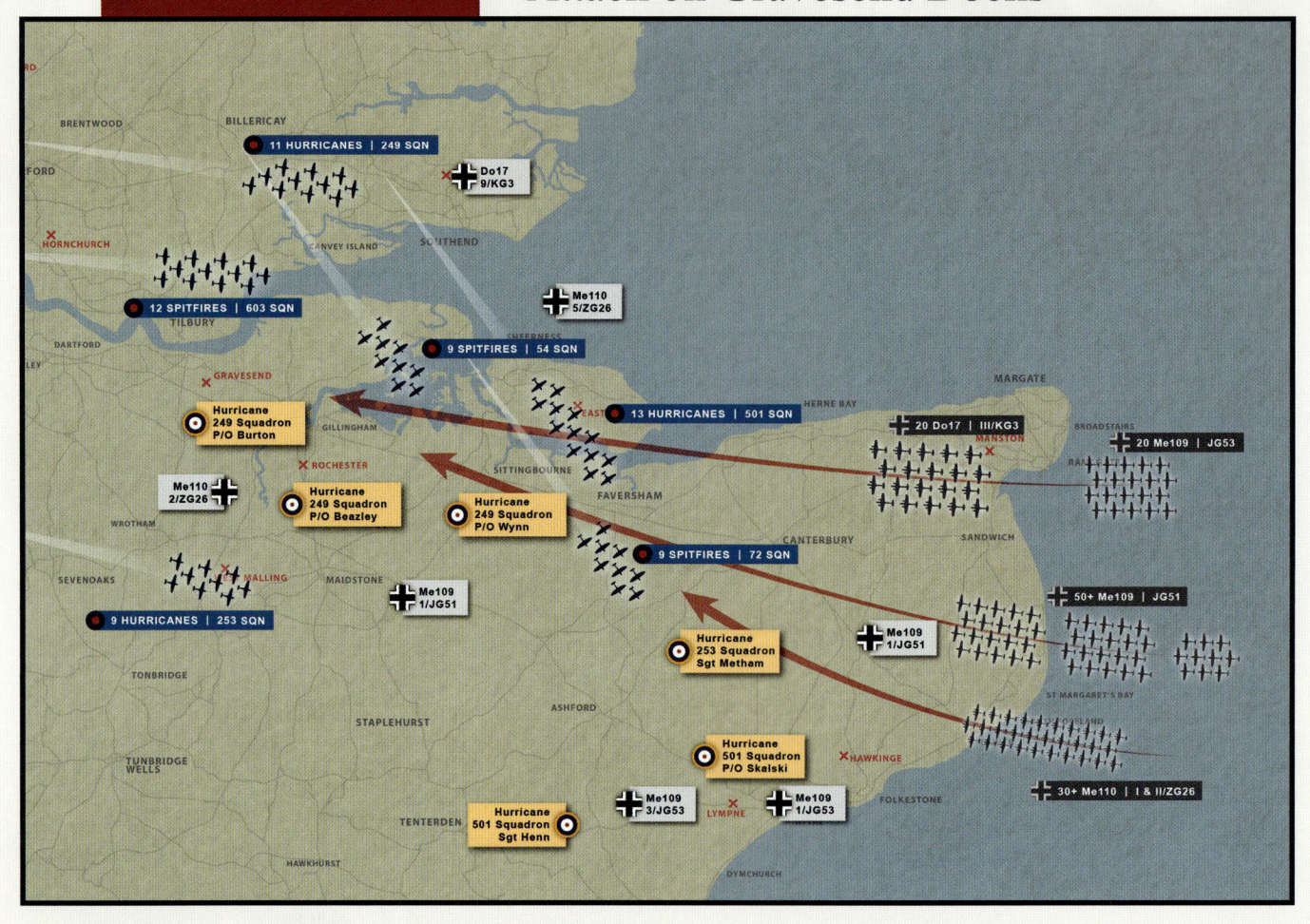

Attack on Gravesend Docks

The pilots of Fighter Command were given no respite by the Luftwaffe. The first raids appeared on the plotting table at 07.15 hours and developed into three distinct threats; two in the Dover Straits and one off North Foreland. Eleven squadrons were scrambled in all, but five were held back to protect their own bases and were not involved in combat, leaving six to meet the enemy.

253 Squadron	- 9 Hurricanes up from Kenley to patrol Hawkinge.
249 Squadron	- 11 Hurricanes up from North Weald to patrol Rochford.
501 Squadron	- 13 Hurricanes up from Gravesend to patrol Dungeness.
54 Squadron	- 9 Spitfires up from Rochford to patrol Chatham.
72 Squadron	- 9 Spitfires up from Croydon to patrol Maidstone.
603 Squadron	- 12 Spitfires up from Hornchurch to patrol Thames Estuary.

The three raids crossed the coast at 07.40 hours, two between Folkestone and Dover and the other over North Foreland, all heading towards the Thames Estuary near Gravesend. Although Fighter Command had reacted quickly to the threat and had squadrons in place, the low cloud at only 3,000 feet and generally overcast conditions 'blinded' the Observer Corps and no accurate track of the enemy could be reported. 253 Squadron was first to engage when they encountered Do17s, Me110s and Me109s south of North Foreland. The raid pressed on and were next engaged by 54 Squadron near Chatham.
The two formations that crossed the coast between Folkestone and Dover also headed across Kent towards Gravesend, but were engaged short of Maidstone by 501, 72 and 249 Squadrons.

Both raids reached the Gravesend and Chatham area where a considerable number of bombs fell randomly. As the force retired 603 Squadron took on Me109s near Canterbury and finally a small attack was made on Lympne where about 30 bombs exploded in the surrounding area.

Luftwaffe Summary:
08.05 hrs. Gravesend attacked with 3 x SC250, 3 x Flambo 250, 130 x SC50, 90 x SD50.

RAF & Luftwaffe Victory Claims

2 September 1940 - 07.45 - 08.15 hrs Combat A. Attack on Gravesend Docks.

RAF Victory Claims			07.45 – 08.15 hrs
253 Sqn	P/O A A G Trueman	Me109 damaged	Rochester
54 Sqn	S/Ldr J A Leathart	Me109 destroyed	Chatham
54 Sqn	F/O G D Gribble	Me109 probable	Chatham
54 Sqn	P/O D A P McMullen	Me109 probable	Chatham
54 Sqn	P/O C F Gray	Me109 destroyed	Chatham
54 Sqn	Sgt R H Robbins	Do215 damaged	Chatham
501 Sqn	F/O S Witorzenc	Do17 destroyed	Ashford
501 Sqn	P/O S Skalski	Me109 destroyed	Ashford
501 Sqn	P/O S Skalski	Me109 destroyed	Ashford
501 Sqn	P/O H C Adams	Me109 destroyed	Ashford
501 Sqn	Sgt J H Lacey	Me109 destroyed	Ashford
501 Sqn	Sgt J H Lacey	Do215 damaged	Ashford
501 Sqn	Sgt P C P Farnes	He113 damaged	Ashford
72 Sqn	F/Sgt H Steere	Me110 damaged	3m south of Chatham
72 Sqn	Sgt W T E Rolls	Me110 destroyed	Maidstone
72 Sqn	Sgt W T E Rolls	Do17 destroyed	Maidstone
72 Sqn	Sgt J White	Do17 destroyed	Maidstone
72 Sqn	Sgt M Gray	Do17 probable	Maidstone
72 Sqn	Sgt J S Gilders	Do17 damaged	south of Maidstone
249 Sqn	S/Ldr J Grandy	Do17 damaged	Canterbury
249 Sqn	F/Lt D G Parnall	Me110 damaged	Rochester
249 Sqn	F/Lt R A Barton	Do17 destroyed	Thames Estuary - Rochford
249 Sqn	P/O J R B Meaker	- shared -	
249 Sqn	P/O P R F Burton	Do17 probable	north of Canterbury
249 Sqn	P/O J R B Meaker	Do17 damaged	Canterbury
249 Sqn	P/O H J S Beazley	Me110 probable	Canterbury
603 Sqn	F/O G J E Haig	Me109 destroyed	north of Hawkinge
603 Sqn	P/O R H Hillary	Me109 destroyed	north of Hawkinge
603 Sqn	P/O R Berry	Me109 destroyed	Hawkinge
603 Sqn	F/O B J G Carbury	Me109 destroyed	off Margate
603 Sqn	Sgt J Stokoe	Me110 damaged	north of Hawkinge

F/O S Witorzenc 501 Sqn

P/O J R B Meaker 249 Sqn

Luftwaffe Victory Claims			07.45 – 08.15 hrs
St I/JG51	Oblt Ernst Terry	Spitfire	
1/JG51	Fw Oskar-Heinz Bär	Spitfire	Canterbury
1/JG51	Lt Erwin Fleig	Spitfire	5km east of Canterbury
2/JG51	Hptm Ernst Wiggers	Hurricane	
2/JG51	Lt Erich Meyer	Hurricane	
9/JG51	Uffz Kurt Koch	Hurricane	
3/JG53	Hptm Wolfgang Lippert	Hurricane	
3/JG53	Ofw Erich Kuhlmann	Spitfire	

Below: The Me109 as flown by Fw Oskar-Heinz Bär of 1/JG51.

37

Contemporary Accounts 253 & 501 Sqns

2 September 1940 - 07.45 - 08.15 hrs Combat A. Attack on Gravesend Docks.

253 SQUADRON INTELLIGENCE REPORT

07.37 hours to 09.00 hours.

9 Hurricanes took off Kenley 07.27 to patrol Hawkinge and then intercept Raid 49. Squadron climbed to 20,000 feet and sighted formation of 20 to 30 bombers 10 miles south of Manston at 17,000 feet escorted by 20 Me109s and possibly He113s. Squadron did slight shallow dive towards bombers but enemy fighters attacked Hurricanes from above and rear and formation broke up and dived.

Green 2 (P/O Trueman) dived to 6,000 feet and then turned towards Rochester aerodrome when he encountered and attacked an Me109 from the rear delivering an astern attack from slightly above and observed pieces breaking away from the tail plane and fuselage.

8 Hurricanes landed Kenley between 08.25 and 09.00 hours.
Our casualties.   1 Hurricane lost.
                    1 pilot slightly injured (Sgt Metham).

501 SQUADRON INTELLIGENCE REPORT

Engagement of No.501 Sqdn with 30+ Dorniers and 50+ Me109s over Maidstone and Ashford area, on 2.9.40 at 08.00 hours.

13 Hurricanes of No.501 Squadron left Gravesend at 07.30 hours. The squadron flew south over Maidstone and Ashford and sighted a large force of Dorniers in the usual 'vic' formation, this time made up of sections of three with 50 or more Me109s spread out in wide formation coming towards them from the direction of Folkestone. The squadron circled round to attack from beam, but was itself attacked by the 109s, which were above and below. A dog-fight developed and Red 3 after attacking two Me109s over Charing, succeeded in bringing down a Do17. This landed in a road near Newchurch. A 109 shot down by Red 2 landed very near to it.

Blue 1 sighted a force of about 15 bombers and 9 He113s on their way back over Ashford, he attacked the He113s and damaged one of them. Ten Hurricanes returned to Gravesend at 09.05 hours. E/A casualties, 4 Me109s, 1 Do17 destroyed, 1 Me109 probably destroyed, 1 He113, 1 Do17, 1 Do215 damaged.

Own losses Pilot Officer S Skalski force landed at Sellindge (pilot safe), Sgt W B Henn injured (whereabouts still unknown). Two Hurricanes lost.

COMBAT REPORT:
Sgt J H Lacey - Yellow 1, A Flight, 501 Squadron

I was leading Yellow Section of 'A' Flight when 501 Squadron attacked the Me109s escorting Do215s. 3 Me109s had climbed above the flight and, to prevent them diving on the squadron from behind, I also climbed and attacked them.

I was able to get in a good burst of about 5 secs at a red cowled Me109, but the E/A immediately turned and I observed no damage. As I followed it round in the turn, I was unable to bring my guns to bear, but after about 30 secs of circling, the Me109 pilot jumped out and did a delayed drop of about 5,000 ft before opening his parachute. Most of the other Me109s were engaged, so I dived out of the dog-fight and attacked No.5 in the last formation of Do215s. Almost as soon as I opened fire, the Do215 broke out of formation and turned south east with smoke issuing from its starboard engine. I continued to fire until my ammunition was exhausted, when I broke away to observe results. The enemy aircraft lost height rapidly until it reached 5,000 ft, which seemed to be its absolute ceiling on one engine, and then proceeded out to sea towards France, losing height very slowly. I then returned to base and landed.

Contemporary Accounts 54 Sqn

2 September 1940 - 07.45 - 08.15 hrs Combat A. Attack on Gravesend Docks.

54 SQUADRON INTELLIGENCE REPORT

07.41 – 08.40 hours

Nine a/c 54 Squadron left Rochford at 07.41 hours to intercept an enemy raid south of Chatham going towards Hornchurch. The raid consisted of lines of Heinkel bombers with fighters milling behind at a height of from 15,000 to 20,000 feet. The Me109s had white wing tips. 54 Squadron attacked by sections but were split up during the combat. There was intense A.A. fire over the Chatham area which probably turned off the enemy bombers.

Eight aircraft returned to Rochford at 08.40 and one (P/O Gray) to Hornchurch.

COMBAT REPORT:
P/O C F Gray – Green 1, B Flight, 54 Squadron

Whilst flying at 25,000 feet I sighted an Me109 below me at about 20,000 feet, and I dived straight on to it. When almost on top I throttled back and got astern, giving it a long burst from about 50 yards range. Immediately glycol and smoke poured out of the machine. I gave it a second burst and the Me109 burst into flames. At the same time I was attacked by another Me109 which shot my wireless plug out of its socket. This Me109 was using cannon shells. I also noticed a big bomber formation travelling homewards but was unable to attack it.

The Me109s appeared to have white round their wing tips and not yellow previously seen.

COMBAT REPORT:
S/Ldr J A Leathart – Red 1, B Flight, 54 Squadron

Enemy was sighted over Ashford when we were over Sheppey at 20,000 feet. I climbed a further 5,000 feet and attacked No.5 of a Vic of five Me109s. There was no result. I dived away and pulled up vertically under a second formation of five Me109s firing at the flank one with full deflection. He dropped vertically and exploded on hitting the ground south of Chatham.

Below: A 54 Squadron Spitfire starting its engine with the aid of the 'Trolley Acc' which provided electrical power to turn the engine over.

Contemporary Accounts 249 Sqn

2 September 1940 - 07.45 - 08.15 hrs Combat A. Attack on Gravesend Docks.

249 SQUADRON INTELLIGENCE REPORT

At 07.30 hours on 2.9.40, 11 a/c of 249 Squadron took off to patrol Rochford at 15,000 feet and intercept raid 50 and on arriving there they saw about 25 Dornier 17s or 215s in close vics of three at that height. E/A were escorted by a large number of Me110s which followed behind in wide vics of three stepped up to 20,000 feet. Our fighters carried out a beam attack in line astern on the leading bombers before enemy fighters could close round enemy bombers. Another attempt was made to attack enemy bombers but by this time enemy fighters had closed round and individual combats with them took place. Enemy bombers maintained formation.

8 aircraft returned to North Weald, 2 crash-landing on arrival. The combat took place around and between Canterbury and Rochford.

Red 2 (Sgt Beard) caused a Dornier 215 to smoke heavily and saw pieces fall off, e/a dropping to the rear of the formation. This is claimed as a 'probable' but it may be the same e/a as was damaged by S/Ldr Grandy.

Yellow 1 (F/Lt Parnall) also damaged a Me110.

The enemy casualties will be seen to exceed those claimed in the Composite Combat Report. For the categories of our aircraft casualties please see Addendum to C.C.R. (our copy apparently lost in the bombing).

Our casualties: (a) aircraft – 5 (cat 2 or 3)
(b) personnel – P/O Wynn wounded.

Contemporary Accounts 249 Sqn
2 September 1940 - 07.45 - 08.15 hrs Combat A. Attack on Gravesend Docks.

COMBAT REPORT:
S/Ldr J Grandy – A Flight, 249 Squadron

I was leading the squadron on patrol over Eastchurch when we were ordered to intercept large forces of e/a to the south. We sighted them flying north-west from Dover direction, we being at about their height. I ordered line astern and we carried out a beam attack on a formation of mixed bombers and fighters – approximately 30 – 40. These were supported to the rear by over 100 Me110s. At approximately 300 yards I fired one 2 – 3 seconds burst and then broke away underneath formation. Red 2 and 3 report 2 Do215s dropping back with smoke pouring out.

Below: On 1 September 1940, 249 Squadron changed places (and aircraft) with 56 Squadron from Boscombe Down to North Weald. It is widely thought that the squadron didn't bother to change the US code letters to GN for some time. This photo possibly backs that theory up as it must have been taken after 14 September when Albert Lewis (third left), joined the squadron and the Hurricane clearly still has the US codes of 56 Squadron. L-R; P/O P R F Burton (killed 27 September), F/Lt Barton, F/Lt A G Lewis DFC, P/O Crossey, F/O T Neil, P/O John Beazley, S/L John Grandy, P/O George Barclay and F/Lt Keith Lofts.

Contemporary Accounts 249 Sqn

2 September 1940 - 07.45 - 08.15 hrs Combat A. Attack on Gravesend Docks.

COMBAT REPORT:
P/O P R F Burton – Yellow 2, A Flight, 249 Squadron

I was right at the rear of the squadron as we attacked the solid block of bombers. I turned to look at my tail and lost Yellow 1 and I singled out a straggler. I got on his tail and fired at his port engine from 300/250 yards, giving him several short bursts. He turned to port and I aimed at his cockpit, using deflection and I could see my ammunition hitting him. I broke off as I was attacked by some Me110s from behind and above. I evaded them and fired at one which overshot me, but without visible effect. I then resumed my attack on the Dornier, firing again at his port engine from astern. Range 300/250 yards with two 4 seconds bursts. Thick black smoke came from his port engine and he started going down slowly turning all the time towards his damaged engine. By this time he was well out of the formation. I do not think he could have got home.

During the whole engagement I experienced intense return fire from the Dornier, coming apparently from 4+ machine guns firing simultaneously from the top rear of the cockpit. I was hit and glycol fumes filled my cockpit, followed by glycol fluid. As a result my engine cut at 10,000 feet and I had to forced-land near Meopham, Kent, in a field, with my undercarriage up. I do not think my aircraft was very seriously damaged.

I understand a German aircraft crashed just near the scene of the combat.

COMBAT REPORT:
P/O H J S Beazley – Green 1, B Flight, 249 Squadron

I fired broadside on at two Dorniers but without effect. I then wheeled and as I was chasing the bombers I saw a Hurricane being attacked from astern on my right by an Me110. I gave the Me110 a quarter deflection shot from about 250 yards. He did a stall turn to the right, exposing a full underneath plan view, and I gave him a 3 seconds burst. He dived and straightened out and I got astern of him, giving him another 2/3 seconds burst from 300/250 yards range. He then flicked completely over on to his back and started to go down, apparently out of control. I think I must have killed or wounded the pilot when I caught him full plan.

I was hit myself directly afterwards by a cannon shell from an Me110 behind me, and I had to bale out from 13,000 feet. I landed unhurt at Boxley Wood, near Gillingham.

COMBAT REPORT:
F/Lt R A Barton – Blue 1, B Flight, 249 Squadron

I selected a Dornier 215 which had broken formation after our first attack and was flying eastwards on its own. I carried out an astern attack, firing about 10 bursts at both engines and cockpit. No evasive tactics were adopted, but there was a lot of return fire, some of which hit my aircraft. Pieces flew off e/a and I noticed what appeared to be a weight on a piece of wire ejected from e/a, but this did not hit me. E/A gradually lost height. P/O Meaker also attacked this e/a and it crash-landed on Rochford aerodrome, having first caught fire. An occupant baled out at 100 feet and his parachute failed to open in time.

P/O Meaker (Blue 2)

I attacked simultaneously with Blue 1 and when he sat back I did four quarter attacks, two from each side. I fired altogether 2,000 rounds. I confirm his version of the combat given above.

Contemporary Accounts 72 Sqn

2 September 1940 - 07.45 - 08.15 hrs Combat A. Attack on Gravesend Docks.

72 SQUADRON OPERATIONS RECORD BOOK

9 aircraft took off from Croydon at 07.45 flying at 15,000 feet on a course of 110°. E/A consisting of Do17s, Me110s and Me109s were encountered over Maidstone flying at 13,000 feet. The Do17s broke up on seeing our fighters, who then attacked the Me as the Do17s turned for home. In this attack 3 Do17s and 1 Me110 were destroyed and 1 Do17 and 1 Me110 damaged.

COMBAT REPORT:
F/Sgt H Steere — Tennis Leader, 72 Squadron

I was ordered to scramble at 07.40. I took off with 9 aircraft and circled gaining height. I received an order vector 100. I turned on to this course, nearing Chatham. I saw several enemy aircraft indicated by AA fire. I was slightly below these aircraft so I turned slightly right still climbing. The squadron went into line astern on me and I turned left to attack and as I went in an Me110 flew across in front of me firing from his rear gun. I fired at him, he turned left into a spiral and smoke came from his port engine. I followed him down firing, until I saw tracer coming over my port plane. I turned very sharply and 'blacked out'. When I recovered there was nothing in sight and as I had expended all my ammunition I returned and landed at Croydon.

COMBAT REPORT:
Sgt J S Gilders — A Flight, 72 Squadron

While on patrol at 0800 hours on Sept. 2nd 1940, the Squadron consisting of Blue, Green and Red sections was ordered to vector 110 degrees and climb to angels 20. Approaching Maidstone at height of 14,000 feet 30 bandits were sighted coming towards us. As I was acting as rearguard above the leading section I did not attack until the enemy bombers had been turned back by the rest of the squadron. I then attacked a Dornier 17 on the left of the formation, which was away from the rest of the bomber formation with another one. I attacked from dead astern and about 1,000 feet above. I gave a preliminary burst at about 250 yards range but could not continue closing in as I sighted two Me109's attacking me from astern. I then broke away and returned to base. The Dornier 17 had lots of smoke coming from the starboard engine and left his partner, crossing over and going below the larger formation on his right. I had not time to see whether he continued going down.

COMBAT REPORT:
Sgt M Gray, A Flight, 72 Squadron

At 07.45 hrs on 2-9-40, 72 Squadron was ordered to scramble and fly on a course of 110 degrees, height 15,000 ft.

When approaching Detling from the west a great amount of Anti-Aircraft fire was observed above Maidstone and the squadron altered course towards the barrage. We were then flying about 11,500 ft. when a formation of 30 Dornier 17s were observed approaching us head on. Upon sighting us the bombers turned away from London in a South Easterly direction losing height gradually. The formation leader then carried out an astern attack on the bombers and as I was a little way behind the main body of the formation and a little higher I did not attack at the same time. After the attack by the rest of the formation the bombers turned slightly and came towards myself flying at a height of 12,000 ft in a S.E. direction. I then dived below the leader of the bomber formation and attacked the Dornier 17 flying No. 5 position in the first Vic formation. As soon as I opened fire the Dornier's wheels dropped and black smoke was seen to be coming from its port engine. I then kept on firing until the aircraft broke away from the formation in a slight dive. A Messerschmitt 109 then attacked me from astern and I dived away.

The Dornier 17 was then losing height very slowly in a S.E. direction and I followed it half way across the channel until it was about 1,000 ft over the sea and 8-10 miles from the coast, still losing height.

As all of our A/C had been ordered to land I left the Dornier and landed at Croydon at 08.45 hrs to refuel and rearm.

Luftwaffe Casualties

2 September 1940 - 07.45 - 08.15 hrs Combat A. Attack on Gravesend Docks.

Luftwaffe Casualties	Combat A	07.45 – 08.15 hrs

1/JG51 Me109E-1 Wn.4807   Shot down and crashed at Nethersole Farm, Womenswold, Kent. Ff: Lt Günther Ruttkowski killed. *See report of 54 Squadron.*

1/JG51 Me109E-1 Wn.4850   Set alight in the air and the pilot baled out badly burned. Aircraft fell at Abbey Farm, near Leeds Castle, Kent. Ff: Lt Helmut Thörl injured PoW.
See report of Sgt Lacey, 501 Squadron.

1/JG51 Me109E-4 Wn.3714   White 13+   Fell into the Channel after being damaged. Ff: Fw Heinz Bär rescued by Seenotdienst.

1/JG53 Me109E-1 Wn.3584   White 14+   Crossed the coast over Folkestone in formation with the bombers A Spitfire cut him off from the formation and, as he was the last aircraft and isolated, he made for home. A Spitfire chased him and after a dogfight near the coast the petrol tank was holed so the pilot made a good forced landing on the Small Arms School Ranges, Hythe, Kent. Ff: Uffz Werner Karl slightly wounded PoW. *See reports of 253 and 501 Squadrons.*

3/JG53 Me109E   Wn.6276   Shot down and crashed in flames at Bridge Farm, Bilsington, Kent. Ff: Obltn Hans Riegel killed. *See report of 501 Squadron.*

3/JG53 Me109E-4 Wn.3494 Yellow 11+   Landed after combat near Boulogne, 50% damage. Ff: Uffz Heinrich Leschert wounded.

2/ZG26 Me110D-1 Wn.3309   U8+DK Shot down by four fighters at 16,000 ft. Aircraft fell into White Horse Wood, Birling, Kent. Ff: Fw Karl Schütz killed. Bf: Uffz Herbert Stüwe baled out wounded and captured. *See reports of 72 Squadron.*

5/ZG26 Me110C-4 Wn.3536   3U+GN Flying in formation at 19,000 ft westwards up the Thames Estuary the crew became involved in a dogfight, and claimed to have shot down a Hurricane, but the starboard engine was hit and a further attack stopped the port engine. Fell into the Thames Estuary off the Nore Lightship, Kent, and the crew took to their dinghy. Ff: Ofw Kurt Rochel and Bf: Uffz Willi Schöffler both PoWs. *See reports of 72 and 249 Squadrons.*

5/ZG26 Me110C-4 Wn.3045   3U+BN Crash landing at Wizernes due to engine damage in combat. 100%. Ff: Fw Hans Müller and Bf: Uffz Gerhard Gröhl both wounded.

8/KG3 Do17Z   Returned to St Trond damaged. Hptm Jürgen de Lalande wounded, rest of crew safe.

9/KG3 Do17Z-2   Wn.3629   5K+BT Took off from St. Omer to attack Eastchurch. Shot down and crash landed on Rochford aerodrome, Essex. Ff: Obltn Ullrich Rohr, Bo: Fw Otto Sprink and Bf: Uffz Karl Seidel all wounded PoWs. Bm: Uffz Kurt Hilbrecht killed. *See report of F/Lt Barton, 249 Squadron.*

9/KG3 Do17Z-3 Wn.3390 5K+GT   Crash landing due to damage at St Omer. 65%. Crew safe.

9/KG3 Do17Z-2 5K+MT Belly landing due to AA damage 16 km SW of Hasselt near St Inglevert, 100%. Sonderführer Klaus Mai of Lw.Kr.Ber.Kp. killed. Ff: Uffz Hans Riedel broke both legs, Bo: Gefr Karl Kindler badly wounded hand. Bf: Ogefr Hans Steinadler slightly wounded.

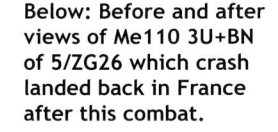

Below: Before and after views of Me110 3U+BN of 5/ZG26 which crash landed back in France after this combat.

COMBAT B

12.40 - 13.45 hrs... Kent
Attack on Eastchurch and Detling

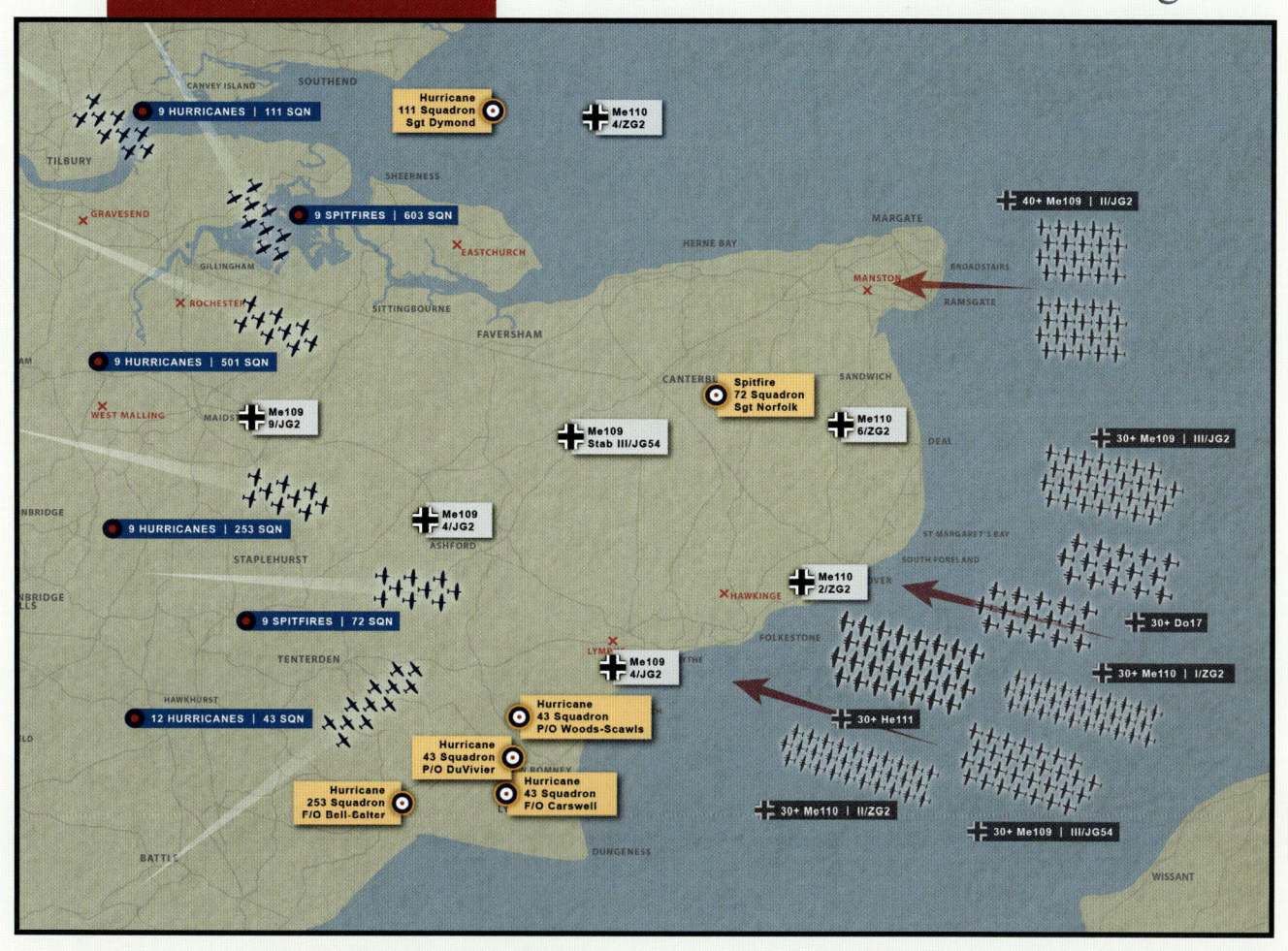

Attack on Eastchurch and Detling

The early morning attack was not followed up and it was midday before another formation was plotted forming over the Channel. These raids followed a similar pattern to the earlier attack and also made for the Gravesend and Chatham area. At 12.20 hours an estimated 50 aircraft crossed the coast over Hythe and headed again for Gravesend by way of Ashford. Then at 12.30 hours a further 100 aircraft in three waves came over Dover, and finally 40 aircraft crossed North Foreland.

Again Fighter Command reacted by scrambling eleven squadrons, six of which remained over the airfields and did not engage the enemy. Four squadrons were ordered to intercept:

72 Squadron - 9 Spitfires up from Croydon to patrol Dover.
46 Squadron - 12 Hurricanes up from Stapleford Tawney (did not engage).
111 Squadron - 9 Hurricanes up from Castle Camps to patrol Rochford.
603 Squadron - 9 Spitfires up from Hornchurch.
253 Squadron - 9 Hurricanes up from Kenley to patrol Maidstone.

72 Squadron was the first to engage when it met 30 Do17s with their Me110 and Me109 escort near Hythe. 603 Squadron then met the same force near Chatham, followed by 111 Squadron.
By 13.00 hours a further six squadrons were scrambled, four to patrol their own airfields and two to intercept:
501 Squadron - 9 Hurricanes up from Gravesend to patrol Maidstone.
43 Squadron - 12 Hurricanes up from Tangmere to patrol Maidstone.

Two RAF airfields were bombed, Eastchurch at 13.10 hours and Detling at 13.15. At Eastchurch a 'lucky' hit set off the bomb dump where a number of 250 lb bombs exploded causing a great deal of damage to buildings and destroying five aircraft.

Luftwaffe Summary:
12.33 hrs. Eastchurch attacked with 15 x SC250, 15 x LLZ250, 180 x SC50, 180 x SD50, 96 x BSK. Buildings and hangars hit, 4 aircraft seen burning on the ground.

13.20 hrs. Detling attacked with 48 x SD50. Buildings and hangars hit.

RAF & Luftwaffe Victory Claims

2 September 1940 - 12.40 - 13.45 hrs Combat B. Attack on Eastchurch and Detling.

RAF Victory Claims		Combat B	12.40 - 13.45 hrs
72 Sqn	S/Ldr A R Collins	Do17 probable	Herne Bay
72 Sqn	S/Ldr A R Collins	Me110 probable	Herne Bay
72 Sqn	F/Lt E Graham	Me110 damaged	Herne Bay
72 Sqn	F/O J W Villa	Me110 destroyed	Herne Bay
72 Sqn	F/O J W Villa	Me110 probable	Herne Bay
72 Sqn	F/O J W Villa	Me110 damaged	Herne Bay
72 Sqn	F/O J W Villa	Me110 damaged	Herne Bay
72 Sqn	F/Sgt H Steere	Me110 destroyed	Canterbury
72 Sqn	Sgt N R Norfolk	Me110 damaged	Canterbury
72 Sqn	Sgt B Douthwaite	Do17 probable	Herne Bay
111 Sqn	F/Lt D C Bruce	Me110 damaged	Thames Estuary
111 Sqn	F/Lt D C Bruce	He111 destroyed	6m east of Chatham
111 Sqn	Sgt R J W Brown	- shared -	
111 Sqn	F/O B H Bowring	He111 probable	10m east of Chatham
111 Sqn	F/O B H Bowring	Me110 damaged	10m east of Chatham
111 Sqn	P/O R J Ritchie	He111 probable	Sheppey
	unknown fighter	- shared -	
111 Sqn	P/O P J Simpson	He111 damaged	10m west of Chatham
111 Sqn	Sgt C E Hampshire	Me110 probable	Thames Estuary
111 Sqn	Sgt R J W Brown	Me109 damaged	6m east of Chatham
111 Sqn	Sgt V H Ekins	Do17 damaged	Thames Estuary
603 Sqn	S/Ldr G L Denholm	Me109 damaged	5m east of Sheppey
603 Sqn	P/O J S Morton	Me109 destroyed	5m east of Sheppey
603 Sqn	F/Lt F W Rushmer	Do17 destroyed	5m east of Sheppey
603 Sqn	P/O R H Hillary	Me109 destroyed	5m east of Sheppey
603 Sqn	P/O R H Hillary	Me109 damaged	5m east of Sheppey
43 Sqn	F/Lt R C Reynell	Me109 destroyed	Lympne
43 Sqn	Sgt J W Jeffreys	Me109 destroyed	Manston
43 Sqn	Sgt J W Jeffreys	Me109 probable	Manston

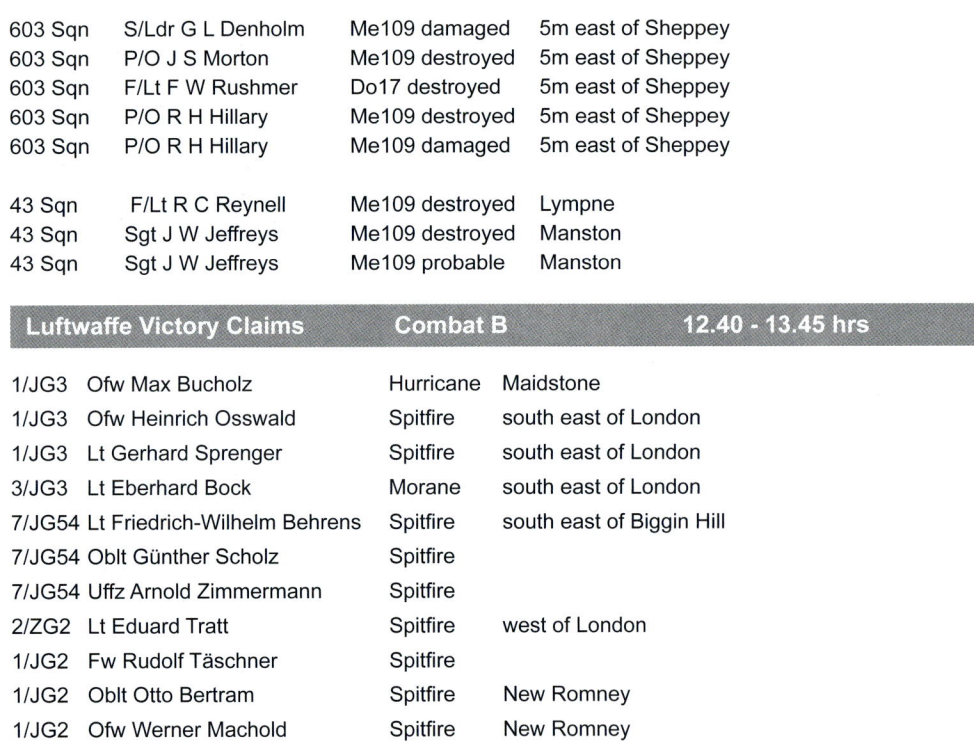

Luftwaffe Victory Claims		Combat B	12.40 - 13.45 hrs
1/JG3	Ofw Max Bucholz	Hurricane	Maidstone
1/JG3	Ofw Heinrich Osswald	Spitfire	south east of London
1/JG3	Lt Gerhard Sprenger	Spitfire	south east of London
3/JG3	Lt Eberhard Bock	Morane	south east of London
7/JG54	Lt Friedrich-Wilhelm Behrens	Spitfire	south east of Biggin Hill
7/JG54	Oblt Günther Scholz	Spitfire	
7/JG54	Uffz Arnold Zimmermann	Spitfire	
2/ZG2	Lt Eduard Tratt	Spitfire	west of London
1/JG2	Fw Rudolf Täschner	Spitfire	
1/JG2	Oblt Otto Bertram	Spitfire	New Romney
1/JG2	Ofw Werner Machold	Spitfire	New Romney
1/JG2	Ofw Werner Machold	Spitfire	New Romney
2/JG52	Oblt Helmut Bennemann	Spitfire	Canterbury
2(J)LG2	Oblt Herbert Ihlefeld	Spitfire	Eynsford

F/O J W Villa 72 Sqn

Sgt R J W Brown 111 Sqn

Sgt V H Ekins 111 Sqn

F/Lt F W Rushmer 603 Sqn

48

Contemporary Accounts 72 Sqn

2 September 1940 - 12.40 - 13.45 hrs Combat B. Attack on Eastchurch and Detling.

72 SQUADRON INTELLIGENCE REPORT

12.06 – 12.53 hours.

Nine Spitfires of No.72 Squadron took off from Croydon at 12.06 hours to patrol behind Dover at 15,000 feet. They were flying in three sections, Red three aircraft leading in vic formation followed by two aircraft (Blue) and a rear guard of four aircraft (Green).

The enemy were first sighted at 12.40 hours flying west over Herne Bay at 20,000 feet. The enemy aircraft consisted of Do17s, Me109s and Me110s. The bombers were flying in tight vic formation, approximately nine to a vic, line astern with the Me109s on their port flank and the Me110s astern and to their left flank.

Red and Blue Section were ordered into line astern and a No.3 astern quarter attack was delivered in a steep dive. Fire was opened at 400 yards, closing to 50 yards, in bursts of from two seconds upwards. Green Section then came into the attack. Green 1 attacked one of about 24 Me110s which had now gone into two defensive circles. Green 2 followed, and states one Me110 opened fire long before he was in range. The enemy formation then broke up, and individual attacks followed. As a result of these attacks one Me110 destroyed, two Do17s and Me110 probable and four Me110s damaged.

Five aircraft landed at Hawkinge at 14.00 hours.

COMBAT REPORT:
S/Ldr A R Collins – Tennis Leader, Red Section, 72 Squadron

I was in Red Section with 3 a/c, Blue Section 2 a/c and Green Section 4 a/c. The latter section acting as rear guard flying in pairs above and behind each flank. I was ordered to patrol behind Dover at 15,000 feet but it was not until 12.40 when I was at 24,000 feet that I saw the enemy formation flying west over Herne Bay at 20,000 feet. The bombers were flying in tight vic approximately 9 to a vic and the vics were in line astern. The 109s were on their right flank and the 110s were behind and on the left flank. I ordered Red and Blue Sections into line astern and delivered a No.3 astern quarter in a steep dive. I opened fire at approximately 400 yards closing to 50 yards at the leading aircraft of the 2nd vic of bombers but although I saw bullets going into his cockpit there was no apparent effect. I broke away in my dive and pulled up behind the outside aircraft of the leading vic of bombers – giving him short bursts into the engines. One engine caught on fire and the other started smoking and he dived down towards the sea. I did not see him hit as I was attacked by four Me110s receiving cannon shells in each mainplane. I turned towards one of them and attacked from head on giving him the rest of my rounds. Smoke came from both engines and he dived down vertically. I did not see him crash as I was busy disengaging myself from the other 3 Me110s. I finally landed at Hawkinge which was our forward base.

COMBAT REPORT:
Sgt B Douthwaite – Red 2, A Flight, 72 Squadron

I took off from Hawkinge as Red 2 on Squadron Leader, and we climbed up on patrol inland of Dover. After reaching 24,000 feet we sighted e/a on our starboard, with AA fire around them. The e/a were proceeding up the Thames Estuary in formations echelon starboard of about 7 aircraft. Leader put Red Section into line astern and we dived on e/a's port bows. After firing without result I lost leader and pulled up and attacked another enemy formation head-on in a dive. I fired at the formation leader, who pulled up and climbed head-on towards me. I continued my fire and saw his port motor start to blaze. He passed out 15 feet underneath me. I then turned to port and attacked an Me109 who was turning steeply to port. I could easily out turn him and fired until he broke away in a steep left-hand dive and I had expended my ammunition. I did not follow him but returned to Hawkinge. I was hit 7 times, and my starboard tyre was punctured, and my starboard flap and gun pipes severed. Also fabric was torn off my port elevator.

49

COMBAT C

16.30 - 17.15 hrs... Kent
Attack on Hornchurch and Eastchurch

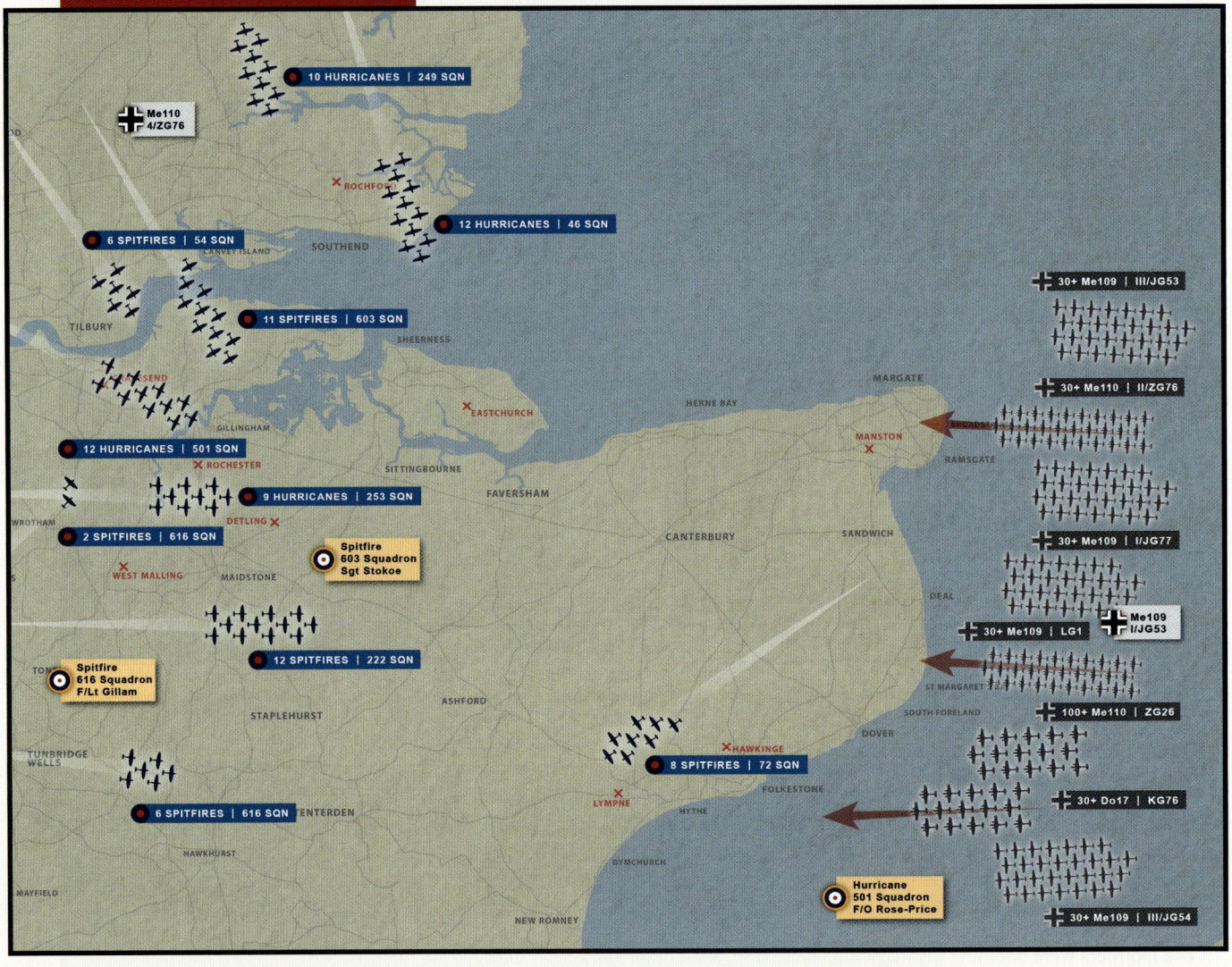

2 SEPTEMBER

Attack on Hornchurch and Eastchurch
The third major attack of the day was first detected at 15.45 hours and crossed the coast in three formations at 16.15 hours over Dungeness, Deal and North Foreland. The raiders set course once again across Kent to the Thames Estuary. Eight squadrons were scrambled to meet the threat:

249 Squadron - 10 Hurricanes up from North Weald to patrol Rochford.
72 Squadron - 8 Spitfires up from Hawkinge to patrol Dungeness.
85 Squadron - 6 Hurricanes up from Croydon (did not engage).
222 Squadron - 12 Spitfires up from Hornchurch to patrol Canterbury.
603 Squadron - 11 Spitfires up from Hornchurch to patrol base.
253 Squadron - 9 Hurricanes up from Kenley to patrol Maidstone. (did not engage).
616 Squadron - 6 Spitfires up from Kenley to patrol base.
54 Squadron - 6 Spitfires up from Hornchurch to patrol base.
242 Squadron - 9 Hurricanes up from Duxford (did not engage).
46 Squadron - 12 Hurricanes up from Stapleford Tawney to patrol North Weald. (did not engage).
501 Squadron - 12 Hurricanes up from Gravesend to patrol base.

72 Squadron was first to sight the enemy while still off the coast of Dungeness and again identified, Do17s with Me110 and Me109 escorts. This time the Do17s were from KG76 escorted by Me110s from I, II and III/ZG26 as well as II/ZG76. Me109s came from III/JG53, III/JG54, I/JG77 and LG1. The morning's clouds had cleared and the raid was closely followed by the Observer Corps as it made its way past Biggin Hill and Hornchurch towards North Weald, then it turned back on itself and attacked Hornchurch. Of the estimated 100 bombs dropped, only six fell within the airfield boundary. Only after Hornchurch was bombed did 603 Squadron spot the bombers and dive on them from 23,000 feet. The raid then split up on its withdrawal. Part turned east and flew out along the Thames Estuary, where 54 Squadron went into combat, and the rest fought their way back over Kent.
Other than the Hornchurch raid bombers had been wandering all over Kent, seemingly aimlessly, scattering bombs. The only other focused attack was made by 12 bombers on Eastchurch after an attack on them by 249 Squadron had been beaten off by Me109s.

Luftwaffe Summary:
16.00 hrs. Hornchurch attacked with 300 x SC50 and SD50. Fires observed.

RAF & Luftwaffe Victory Claims

2 September 1940 - 16.30 - 17.15 hrs Combat C. Attack on Hornchurch and Eastchurch

RAF Victory Claims		Combat C	16.30 - 17.15 hrs
603 Sqn	P/O R H Hillary	Me109 probable	Hornchurch
603 Sqn	P/O D Stewart-Clarke	Me110 probable	Hornchurch
501 Sqn	P/O J A A Gibson	Do17 damaged	Dungeness
501 Sqn	F/Sgt P F Morfill	Do17 damaged	Dungeness
501 Sqn	Sgt J H Lacey	Me109 destroyed	Dungeness
501 Sqn	Sgt P C P Farnes	Me109 damaged	Dungeness
616 Sqn	F/Lt D E Gillam	Me110 destroyed	Maidstone
616 Sqn	Sgt J Hopewell	Me110 destroyed	Maidstone
72 Sqn	P/O E E Males	Me110 damaged	Dungeness
72 Sqn	P/O N C H Robson	Me110 damaged	Dungeness
72 Sqn	Sgt B Douthwaite	Me110 damaged	Dungeness
72 Sqn	Sgt B Douthwaite	Me110 damaged	Dungeness
222 Sqn	F/Lt A I Robinson	Me109 destroyed	Maidstone - Gravesend
222 Sqn	Sgt S Baxter	Me110 probable	Maidstone - Gravesend
222 Sqn	Sgt S Baxter	Me110 damaged	Maidstone - Gravesend
222 Sqn	Sgt S Baxter	Do17 damaged	Maidstone - Gravesend
54 Sqn	P/O D A P McMullen	Do215 destroyed	Hornchurch
54 Sqn	P/O E F Edsall	Do215 damaged	Hornchurch
54 Sqn	Sgt R H Robbins	Me109 destroyed	Hornchurch
249 Sqn	F/Lt D G Parnall	Me110 destroyed	5m south of Billericay
249 Sqn	F/Lt D G Parnall	Me110 damaged	Thames Estuary
249 Sqn	P/O J R B Meaker	Me110 destroyed	Gravesend
249 Sqn	P/O R G A Barclay	Me110 damaged	Thames Estuary
249 Sqn	Sgt H J Davidson	Me110 destroyed	Sutton Valence

Sgt J Hopewell 616 Sqn

P/O D A P McMullen 54 Sqn

F/Lt D G Parnall 249 Sqn

Ogfr Karl-Heinz Boock 7/ZG26

Luftwaffe Victory Claims		Combat C	16.30 - 17.15 hrs
7/JG53	Fw Herbert Schramm	Spitfire	north east of Dungeness
7/JG53	Fw Werner Stumpf	Spitfire	north east of Dungeness
7/JG54	Fw Erwin Leykauf	Spitfire	Dover-Folkestone
9/JG54	Oblt Richard Hausmann	Hurricane u/c	
St I/JG77	Oblt Herbert Kunze	Spitfire	
3/JG77	Uffz Rudolf Meixner	Spitfire	
13(Z)/LG1	Lt Karl Goetze	Spitfire	London
St/ZG76	Genlt Walter Grabmann	Spitfire	
St/ZG76	Genlt Walter Grabmann	Spitfire	
St II/ZG76	Uffz Georg Hommel Bs	Spitfire	east of London
St II/ZG76	Oblt E-H v Schlotheim	Spitfire	east of London
St II/ZG76	Oblt E-H v Schlotheim	Spitfire	north east of London
4/ZG76	Uffz Fritz Auerbach (Bf)	Spitfire	south of London
5/ZG26	Ofw Kurt Rochel	Hurricane	Thames Estuary
5/ZG76	Oblt Hortari Schmude	Spitfire	
5/ZG76	Oblt Wilhelm Hobein	Spitfire	
5/ZG76	Oblt Hortari Schmude	Spitfire	south of London
5/ZG76	Uffz Johann Horst	Spitfire	Tonbridge
6/ZG76	Oblt Wilhelm Herget	Spitfire	London
III/ZG26	Oblt Günther Tonne	Unknown	
7/ZG26	Uffz Rudolf Eiberg (Bf)	Spitfire	
7/ZG26	Ogfr Karl-Heinz Boock	Spitfire	Thames Estuary
9/ZG76	Fw Hans Peterburs	Fighter	
9/ZG76	Fw Hans Peterburs	Fighter	

59

Of course, the tally of Luftwaffe aircraft falling on English soil was only half the story. Every day German fighters and bombers would return with varying amounts of damage, sometimes being written off or, at the very least, being put out of action for some time.
This Me110 3U+BR of 7/ZG26 was damaged in combat on 2 September and landed back at Arques with a wounded pilot. Assessed as having 45% damage, it was dismantled and loaded onto a small barge heading for a repair facility. So although many RAF pilot's claims don't seem to have a definite victim, their efforts may well have produced this sort of result.

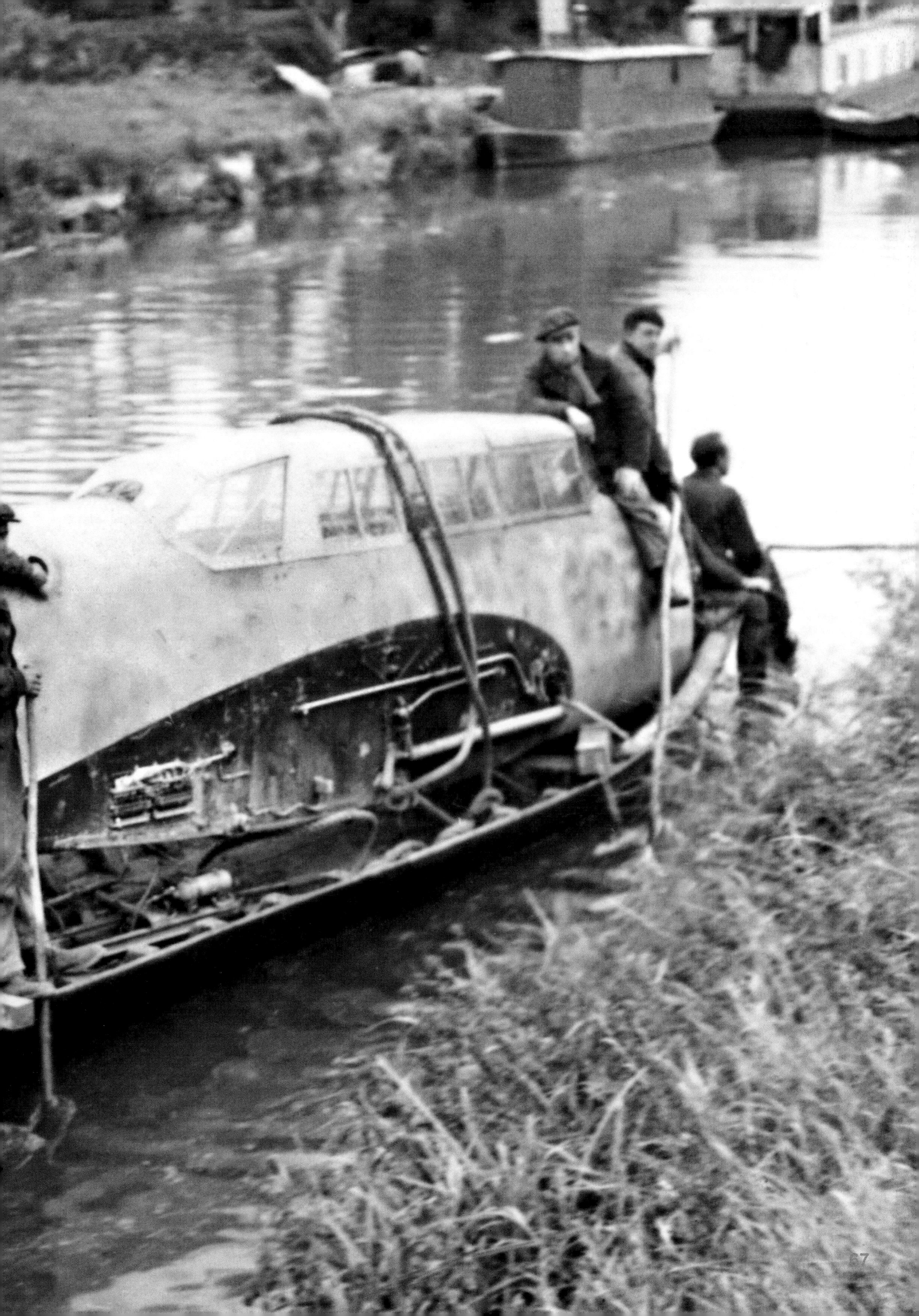

2 SEPTEMBER

COMBAT D 16.35 hrs... off Yarmouth

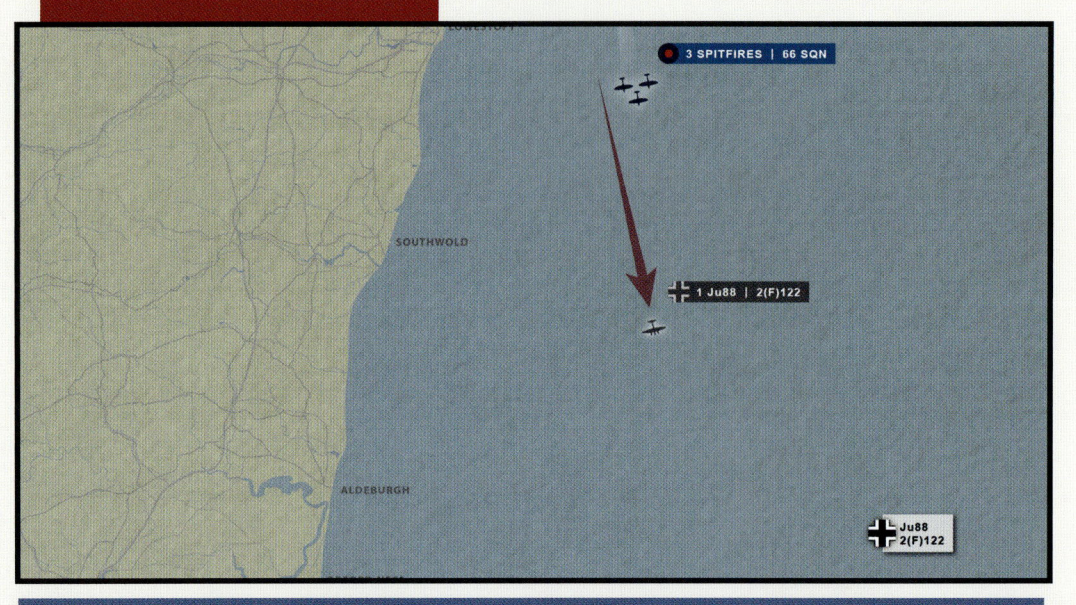

RAF Victory Claims		Combat D	16.35 hrs
66 Sqn	P/O R J Mather	Ju88 destroyed	north east of Smiths Knoll
66 Sqn	P/O C A W Bodie	- shared -	
66 Sqn	Sgt D A C Hunt	- shared -	

Luftwaffe Casualty	Combat D	16.35 hrs

2(F)/122   Ju88A-1   Wn.0276   F6+DK   Fell into the sea 70 miles east of Aldeburgh during a reconnaissance flight. Bo: Oblt Siegfried Schmid, Ff: Fw Bruno Jahnke, Bf: Ogefr Hans Rockstroh and Bs: Gefr Joseph Kronberg all missing.

66 SQUADRON INTELLIGENCE REPORT

Red Section 66 were ordered up at 16.10 hours and given a vector of 150 degrees at 10,000 feet. At 16.35 a vector of 010 bandit ahead was given. At 16.36 hours Red Section was about 20 miles east of Yarmouth, when 'Tallyho' was given by Red 3 who sighted e/a proceeding north about 2 miles ahead at 20,000 feet.

Red 1 (P/O R J Mather) saw e/a do a gentle turn on to south-east course and go into a shallow dive at approximately 310 m.p.h. Red 1 after about 10 minutes opened fire from astern from 400 to 200 yards firing 3 bursts totalling 10 seconds after which Red 1 broke away experiencing fairly accurate machine gun fire from e/a. During this time Red 2 and 3 engaged the enemy and broke away. Red 1 came in again and opened fire from astern using up all ammunition in 3 bursts. E/A passed through some broken cumulus cloud at 8,000 feet but made no use of it and continued to dive to sea level where he flew for a short while on his starboard engine before hitting the water. E/A remained afloat for about 10 seconds before disappearing. A collapsible yellow rubber boat appeared upside down and also a white wooden box and three bodies floating in the water which showed no sign of life. Position at which e/a hit water was approximately 70 miles east of Aldeburgh. Weather was clear above 6,000 feet with some cloud at 8,000 feet and some at 25,000. Below 6,000 feet rather hazy.

Red 2 (P/O H C Bodie) followed Red leader and took up a position about 50 yards to the right and behind Red 1. When Red 1 broke off Red 2 came up and fired 3 bursts of 2 seconds each between 300 – 150 yards then broke and climbed and turned in and went from quarter to astern firing 3 more short bursts of 2 seconds and broke away again waiting whilst Red 1 and Red 3 attacked, then Red 2 gave another burst noticing that the return fire had ceased entirely and port engine of e/a was emitting puffs of white smoke and at times a long stream of it. E/A carried on level for some time, Red 2 then closed to about 100 yards and gave a 4 seconds burst and broke to port observing e/a crash into the sea.

Red 3 (Sgt D A C Hunt) observing Red 1 and Red 2 breaking away from e/a, came in from starboard quarter developing into a stern attack firing a burst of 8 seconds from 350 to 250 yards. During this attack experienced a very sporadic return fire from single machine gun in normal upper gun position. Red 3 breaking away and waiting opportunity gave a second stern attack, little return fire being noticed. Red 3 having used all ammunition broke away to safe distance. No deflection allowance made. No slipstream effect.

Red 1 fired 2320 rounds span 60 feet, 2 stoppages, one: premature explosion, 2 misfires. A/c found u/s on landing owing to e/a fire.

Red 2 fired 2211 rounds, span 60 feet, no stoppages. A/c found u/s on landing owing to e/a fire.

Red 3 fired 2163 rounds, no stoppages. R/T worked satisfactorily except in the case of Red 2 which was bad on the way to home base. No cine gun carried. Red 1, 2 and 3 landed together at 17.35 hours.

17.00 - 17.45 hrs... Kent – Attack on Eastchurch   COMBAT E

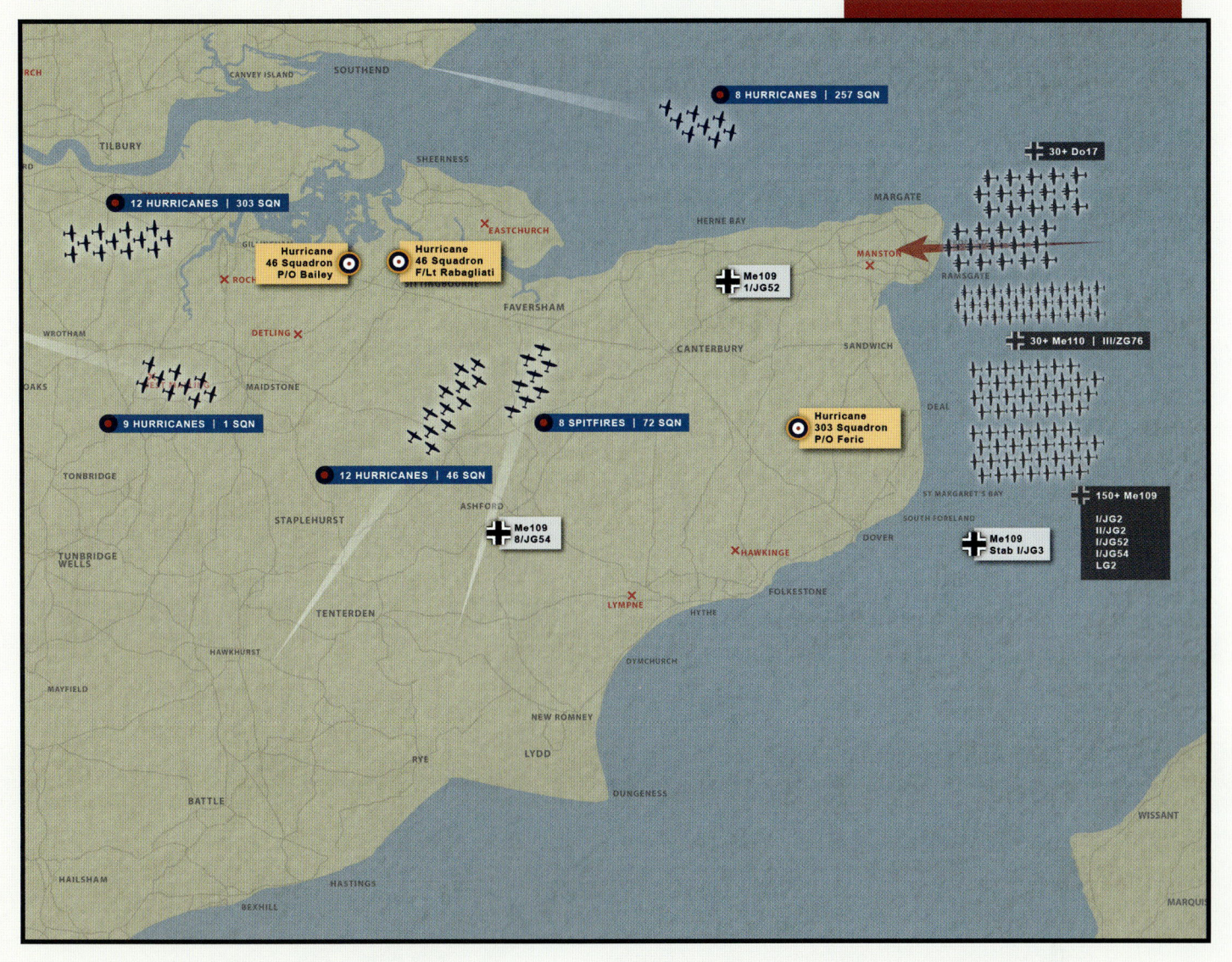

Attack on Eastchurch
Just as the earlier raid (Combat C) headed back across the Channel, a further raid appeared crossing North Foreland. A number of enemy aircraft had remained over the Channel during the day, to confuse Fighter Command as to which plot was a genuine threat, and a few other aircraft crossed the Kent coast only to immediately turn around and head back over the Channel. Me110s from III/ZG76 and Me109s from I and II/JG2, I/JG52, I/JG54 and LG2 escorted the Do17s to Eastchurch.

72 and 46 Squadrons had not landed after the earlier raid and were still on patrol. Three further squadrons were scrambled to relieve them:
303 Squadron - 12 Hurricanes up from Northolt to patrol Chatham.
257 Squadron - 8 Hurricanes up from Martlesham Heath to patrol East Mersea.
85 Squadron - 6 Hurricanes up from Croydon (did not engage).
501 Squadron - 7 Hurricanes up from Biggin Hill (did not engage).
1 Squadron - 9 Hurricanes up from Northolt to patrol base.

72 Squadron was first to intercept the raid near Herne Bay, then 46 Squadron just before the bombers reached their target which again turned out to be the Coastal Command airfield at Eastchurch. As the raid retired 303 and 257 Squadrons also engaged. Following the concerted attacks of the previous few hours, and the many earlier raids, administrative and medical staff were relocated outside of the airfield, which was badly cratered and its buildings all severely damaged.

Luftwaffe Summary:
17.15 hrs. Eastchurch attacked with 19 SC500 and 4 Flambo 250. Building and hangars hit.

RAF & Luftwaffe Victory Claims

2 September 1940 - 17.00 - 17.45 hrs Combat E. Attack on Eastchurch

RAF Victory Claims		Combat E	17.00 - 17.45 hrs
1 Sqn	F/Lt H B L Hillcoat	Me109 probable	10m N Dungeness
1 Sqn	P/O C A C Chetham	Me109 damaged	10m N Dungeness
46 Sqn	P/O C F Ambrose	Me109 destroyed	Eastchurch
	Unknown pilot	shared	
46 Sqn	F/Sgt E E Williams	Do215 damaged	Sheerness - Eastchurch
46 Sqn	Sgt E Bloor	Me109 destroyed	Eastchurch
46 Sqn	Unknown pilot	Me109 probable	Eastchurch - Sheerness
46 Sqn	Unknown pilot	Me109 damaged	Eastchurch - Sheerness
46 Sqn	Unknown pilot	Me109 damaged	Eastchurch - Sheerness
46 Sqn	Unknown pilot	Do215 probable	Eastchurch - Sheerness
257 Sqn	Sgt R C Nutter	Me109 probable	off Ramsgate
303 Sqn	F/O Z Henneberg	Me109 damaged	8m into France
303 Sqn	P/O M Feric	Me109 probable	over French coast
303 Sqn	Sgt J Frantisek	Me109 destroyed	Dover
303 Sqn	Sgt J Rogowski	Me109 destroyed	10m off France
72 Sqn	P/O E E Males	Me109 destroyed	Chatham
72 Sqn	Sgt B Douthwaite	Me109 damaged	Chatham

Fw Erich Rudorffer 1/JG2

Fw Siegfried Schnell 4/JG2

Luftwaffe Victory Claims		Combat E	17.00 - 17.45 hrs
1/JG2	Fw Erich Rudorffer	Hurricane	Faversham
1/JG2	Ofw Werner Machold	Spitfire	Sittingbourne
1/JG2	Oblt Otto Bertram	Spitfire	Eastchurch
4/JG2	Fw Siegfried Schnell	Hurricane	
1/JG52	Oblt Kurt Kirchner	Spitfire	south of Eastchurch
1/JG52	Lt Günter Büsgen	Spitfire	south of Eastchurch
1/JG52	Ofw Oskar Strack	Spitfire	south of Eastchurch
1/JG52	Lt Franz Essl	Hurricane	south of Eastchurch
I./JG52	Oblt Wolfgang Ewald	Spitfire u/c	Eastchurch
I./JG52	Unknown pilot	Spitfire u/c	
I./JG52	Unknown pilot	Spitfire u/c	
1/JG54	Lt Hans Götz	Spitfire	
1/JG54	Lt Hans Götz	Hurricane	
2(J)/LG2	Oblt Herbert Ihlefeld	Spitfire	Sheerness
2(J)/LG2	Ofw Hermann Staege	Spitfire	Sheerness
2(J)/LG2	Ofw Georg Schott	Spitfire	Sheerness
3(J)/LG2	Uffz Otto Riedel	Spitfire -	
1(J)/LG2	Fhr H-J Marseille	Spitfire u/c	Detling
3(J)/LG2	Oblt Adolf Buhl	Spitfire -	

A lot of future Luftwaffe Aces were involved in this combat including the very young Hans Joachim Marseille pictured above.

Contemporary Accounts 1 Sqn
2 September 1940 - 17.00 - 17.45 hrs Combat E. Attack on Eastchurch

1 SQUADRON OPERATIONS RECORD BOOK

In the afternoon 9 Hurricanes led by F/Lt Hillcoat encountered a formation of Me109s at 20,000 feet. In the engagement F/Lt Hillcoat probably destroyed one and P/O Chetham damaged another. Our casualties nil.

COMBAT REPORT:
F/Lt H B L Hillcoat – Blue 1, B Flight, 1 Squadron

I was Blue 1 leading No.1 Squadron. When patrolling base and climbing AA bursts were sighted over London at 18,000 feet. The squadron was then at 10,000 feet, and I started to climb between the sun and the AA bursts. Fresh AA fire showed that the e/a were proceeding south-east. We headed south-east still climbing. Shortly before the coast I saw that the bomber formation was well over the sea, and that there were many fighter formations at different heights covering a wide area, about 12 a/c in each formation flying in line astern in defensive circles. I climbed to 20,000 feet and attacked a formation of Me109s at 19,000 feet on the extreme right of their formation, and they promptly formed a defensive circle, and were joined by other formations. There were also He113s above identified by other pilots. I attacked one Me109. After the first burst, smoke appeared and glycol poured from the radiator. I gave him five or six bursts of two seconds at point blank range about 100 yards, and could see the ammunition hitting him. My attack was from the rear with slight deflection. I broke off when I was satisfied that the e/a could not get home. It went down in a shallow dive about 10 miles inland north of Dungeness, near Ashford. About a dozen Me109s were manoeuvring to get on my tail, so I dived to ground level, and made my way back to base.

Harry Hillcoat's 'probable' 109 was almost certainly this one which force landed at Finns Farm near Ashford in Kent. Black 2 was flown by Uffz Heinrich Elbers who survived with wounds to his foot. His aircraft was subsequently put on display to the British public, this photo (left) was taken in Blackpool.

Contemporary Accounts 257 Sqn

2 September 1940 - 17.00 - 17.45 hrs Combat E. Attack on Eastchurch

257 SQUADRON INTELLIGENCE REPORT

Eight Hurricanes, Blue, Green, Red Sections 257 Squadron left Martlesham 17.15 hours on 2.9.40 to intercept Raid No.6. They were ordered to fly down to East Mersea and to patrol at 15,000 feet. The squadron which was led by F/L Beresford, Red 1, was flying southwards to the north of the Thames Estuary when A.A. fire was noticed around Dover. At this time, about 17.35 hours, the acting squadron leader ordered all sections into line astern. The squadron was then flying at a height of about 17,000 feet. Green 1 (F/O Mitchell), who was leading the last section, then reported sighting enemy aircraft in Eastchurch region. The squadron leader therefore ordered Green 1 to lead on.

The whole squadron then turned to port 180 degrees towards the north, and was flying towards the Thames Estuary when about twenty fighter aircraft passed them on port side, about a quarter of a mile away at the same height flying south. The aircraft which were against the sun were taken by the squadron to be friendly fighters. One or two of these aircraft broke away from the main body, which was not in any formation, and made a port turn. The aircraft were camouflaged in the standard German colouring, but had the tips of their wings painted white to give them a rounded appearance.

As no identifying crosses could be seen, the aircraft were thus still mistaken for friendly fighters. It was only when one of them banked, preparing to make an attack on Red 2, the second a/c from the rear, that Red 3 (Sgt Nutter) who was about 400 yards astern of Red 2, noticed black crosses under the wings. He dived after the e/a and fired a short burst at him. The Me109 immediately flicked into a vertical dive, doing left hand turns.

Red 3, describing the ensuing fight in his combat report, states: 'I opened fire at 300 yards, firing short bursts, and finally closed to about 20 yards'. The e/a dived down with Red 3 on his tail. By this time both aircraft had flown over the sea, off Ramsgate. 'At 1,500 feet', the combat report continues, 'He flicked on his back, and when I last saw him, he was diving almost vertically towards the sea at over 400 m.p.h. I then lost sight of him whilst pulling out of my dive. When last I saw him, glycol was streaming from both his radiators.' The Me109 disappeared into the haze over the sea.

An aircraft was seen at this time by the coastguards near Ramsgate (inquiry via Manston Intelligence) to come out of a dive at about 500 feet and fly towards the east obviously in trouble. In the meantime the rest of the squadron turned on the Me109s which raced out towards the sea, flying east. Some of the e/a encountered AA fire in the Deal region and Blue 1 (P/O Bon-Seigneur) intercepted one of them as it was flying north-east over the sea. He opened fire at 300 yards with a deflection shot of two seconds, closing in, and continued to fire, but he was unable to observe result, although he believes that he damaged the e/a.

The other members of the squadron chased the other e/a out to sea, but were unable to catch them up, and were ordered back to base.

Eight Hurricanes landed Martlesham 18.18.

COMBAT REPORT:
Sgt R C Nutter — Red 3, A Flight, 257 Squadron

Flying as Red 3 at rear of squadron, I saw 12 Me109s approaching, one of which attempted to attack Red 2. I fired a short burst at him and he immediately flicked into a vertical dive doing left hand turns. I opened fire at 300 yards; firing short bursts, and finally closed to about 20 yards. At 1,500 feet he flicked on to his back and when I last saw him, he was diving almost vertically towards the sea at over 400 m.p.h. I then lost sight of him whilst pulling out from my own dive. When last I saw him, glycol was streaming from both his radiators.

Contemporary Accounts 303 Sqn

2 September 1940 - 17.00 - 17.45 hrs Combat E. Attack on Eastchurch

303 SQUADRON INTELLIGENCE REPORT

At 17.50 hours near Dover.

12 Hurricanes took off from Northolt at 17.30 hours to intercept Raid No.6, then Raid No.17, then to patrol Ashford. 11 Hurricanes landed at Northolt 18.35 hours – 18.50 hours. P/O Feric forced landed at Mythorne near Dover at about 18.00 hours.

E/A casualties – 2 Me109s destroyed, 1 probable, 1 damaged.

Our casualties – 1 Hurricane – pilots – nil.

Near Dover the squadron was patrolling at 19,000 feet, Sgts Rogowski and Frantisek Green 2 and 3 were rear guard. Sgt Rogowski saw a formation of 9 Me109s diving on the squadron out of the sun from 22,000 feet. He immediately delivered a head on attack into the formation, breaking it up. The Me109s fell away on both sides, and the surprise was thereby frustrated. Sgt Frantisek, who was further away, engaged the two Me109s nearest to him, and the whole enemy formation scattered and dived for the French coast.

The leading sections of the two flights, Red and Blue, were too far away and unable to take part in the battle, which became a running dog fight over the Channel, with Green and Yellow Sections pursuing individual e/a.

Sgt Rogowski shot down his Me109 ten miles from the French coast in flames into the sea.

Sgt Frantisek's Me109 broke away down left and got on to the tail of Yellow 1, F/O Henneberg, but without hitting him. Sgt Frantisek closed to 100 yards and attacked repeatedly with short bursts. A great cloud of black smoke rose from the Me's engine and it crashed nose down 2/3 km from the sea.

Meanwhile, F/O Henneberg was pursuer as well as pursued. After two bursts at 150 yards, smoke and fire appeared from the starboard side of the Me's engine. He dived lower, and at 3,000 feet, now 8 miles over France, F/O Henneberg closed for the last time, being then compelled to break off and upwards by heavy m/g fire and light flak.

The Polish pilots showed up very well in this action, working in intelligent combination and pressing their attack right home. Sgt Rogowski deserves special commendation for his quick and courageous attack which probably saved the squadron from what might have been a disastrous surprise.

COMBAT REPORT:
Sgt J Rogowski – Green 3, B Flight, 303 Squadron

I was Green 3, rear guard. I saw 9 Me109s approaching at 22,000 feet out of the sun to surprise us. I attacked the formation head on. The e/a broke up and scattered and dived towards France. I followed one and after the 4th burst, his engine caught fire and he crashed into the sea about 10 miles from France. Then I saw P/O Feric in trouble, smoking and gliding so I stayed with him and saw him land and then get out and wave to me from a field about 10 miles north-west of Dover. So I went home.

COMBAT REPORT:
F/O M Feric – Yellow 2, A Flight, 303 Squadron

I was Yellow 2. We sighted nine Me109 west of Dover, and gave chase over the sea at 20,000 ft. I fired a short burst at 250 yds without effect and two more at 150 yds astride the French Coast. E/A turned on his back and dived vertically. As I gave Me a last burst, oil covered my Perspex I pulled out of my dive at 10,000 ft and turned homewards. I opened the hood and smoke was pouring out of my engine. The engine spluttered, shook and throbbed. I thought it might catch fire and tear itself out. I switched off and glided across the Channel with Sgt Rogowski escorting me. I elected a field and landed with undercarriage down, but it was too small and I ran into bushes. The u/c collapsed, airscrew and left wing were smashed and other damage done. Engine was still smoking. I took my papers and parachute etc out of the 'plane. Soldiers came up and after hesitation were convinced I was RAF. I was taken to an R.A. mess, given supper and driven to Northolt at midnight.

73

Contemporary Accounts 46 Sqn

2 September 1940 - 17.00 - 17.45 hrs Combat E. Attack on Eastchurch

2 SEPTEMBER

46 SQUADRON OPERATIONS RECORD BOOK

Whilst on patrol enemy aircraft were intercepted and a dog fight ensued. Some damage was inflicted upon the enemy. F/Lt Rabagliati force landed near Sittingbourne and was uninjured. P/O Bailey was missing from this patrol.

COMBAT REPORT:
P/O C F Ambrose - A Flight, 46 Squadron

Bomber formation: Do215 proceeding NW escorts of 110 and 109 above. Speed not noted.

I lost sight of bomber formation and engaged a 109 which dived towards ground. Some tracer was fired at me from astern but was avoided. On second burst, glycol was seen to pour from enemy's radiator, he slowed up, fire was continued until his speed dropped to approx. 100 mph when he glided through H.T. cables, tearing off hood and was taken into custody on a ploughed field apparently uninjured (S.E. of Herne Bay).

Take off 16.36   Landed 18.00

Below: Pilot Officer Ambrose's victim was this Me109 'White 12' of 1/JG52 flown by Heinz Uerlings. One has to seriously question the centre of gravity calculations for the lorry!

Contemporary Accounts 46 & 72 Sqns

2 September 1940 - 17.00 - 17.45 hrs Combat E. Attack on Eastchurch

COMBAT REPORT:
F/Sgt E E Williams – Green 1, B Flight, 46 Squadron

Bomber formation flying NW, fighter escort of Me109s and 110s above. Dark camouflage, 109s white wing tips with black crosses, light blue over green under surfaces. Do215 dark camouflage with black crosses outlined with white on upper surfaces.

I was leading Green section, the last to attack, in line astern formation and sighted a Do215 turning E. below me, over Eastchurch. I attacked this E/A on the quarter from about 3,000 ft above giving one burst of about 5 secs. Tracer seen entering starboard engine and carried across cockpit into port engine. EA then took evasive action by turning first to port and then starboard, losing height. I saw black smoke coming from starboard engine and A/C apparently slowing up.

I then noticed tracer passing over my cockpit and broke off attack. By this time enemy formation appeared thoroughly disbanded and heading out to sea about 3,000 ft above my level.

Take off 16.36   Landed 17.55

> *I observed an Me109 coming from the starboard side onto No 2's tail. I turned head on to E/A and gave him a 3 sec burst. E/A then turned hard to port showing me all its underside. Gave him a good burst from approximately 50 yds and E/A disappeared. I then had all my work cut out to look for Me109s which were trying to get on my tail. Successfully avoided E/As and returned to base. Green 2 saw the Me109 go down and the starboard side pouring out black smoke apparently out of control. Camouflage on Me109 dark blue wing tips with large black cross. Light blue under surfaces.*
>
> Sgt E Bloor – Green 3, B Flight, 46 Squadron

72 SQUADRON INTELLIGENCE REPORT

17.06 – 18.25 hours.

Six Spitfires of No.72 Squadron took off from Hawkinge to patrol base at 15,000 feet. The formation consisted of four aircraft (Blue Section) leading, with a rear guard of two aircraft. The enemy's presence was indicated by A.A. fire and was sighted over Chatham. It consisted of approximately twenty Do215s and fifty Me109s and Me110s.

On approaching the enemy formation the leader ordered line astern attack and approached the enemy from above and astern, out of the sun. On being attacked, the enemy broke formation, and the Me109s attacked our fighters. Individual attacks then developed and covered Chatham Herne Bay area. Sgt Douthwaite reports he was shot at by an Me109 firing rearwards.

From this engagement one Me109 was destroyed and one Me109 damaged.

COMBAT REPORT:
P/O E E Males – Blue 2, B Flight, 72 Squadron

I was flying Blue 2 in the leading section, with three aircraft weaving behind when about 40 Me109s were sighted to the east. We were slightly below them, and after climbing to their level, during which time they had broken formation and were going round in a circle anti-clockwise. Blue 1 led us in echelon starboard, but I could not get a bead on any enemy a/c. I broke away and climbed into the sun and came down on a 109 from 2,000 feet above. He dived away for the coast and I had difficulty in keeping up with him from 15,000 feet to sea level. I fired several bursts and used all my ammunition while we were flying south at 50 feet over the sea. White smoke came from underneath the engine and 3 large pieces fell off and after about 5 minutes he dived into the sea about 3 miles from the French coast. There was no sign of the pilot or wreckage. The e/a was travelling at about 200 m.p.h. when he went in. The Me109 was painted in a green and grey mottle camouflage. I returned to forward base, flying due north to Dover.

RAF & Luftwaffe Casualties

2 September 1940 - 17.00 - 17.45 hrs Combat E. Attack on Eastchurch

RAF Casualties	Combat E	17.00 - 17.45 hrs

46 Sqn Hurricane P3067   P/O J C L Bailey – killed. Shot down in combat over the Thames Estuary and aircraft crashed at Sittingbourne Golf Links, Sittingbourne, Kent. Body of the pilot taken to Royal Naval Hospital, Chatham, and buried at Maidstone.

46 Sqn Hurricane P3597   F/Lt A C Rabagliati – safe. Forced-landed at Borden near Sittingbourne following combat over Thames Estuary.

303 Sqn Hurricane R4178 RF-G   F/O M Feric – safe. Force-landed between Elvington Village and Lower Eythorne, Kent.

John Cyril Lindsay Dyson Bailey (20)
Born: Stockland, Devon.
Joined 46 Squadron on 20th July 1940.
Combat Claims – none.

Luftwaffe Casualties	Combat E	17.00 - 17.45 hrs

1/JG52 Me109E-4 Wn1261   White 12+   Developed engine trouble during a free-lance patrol with four other aircraft. While making a forced landing at Tile Lodge Farm, Hoath, Kent, it was attacked by a Hurricane. The engine had been hit by 303 bullets. Ff: Fw Heinz Uerlings PoW. *See report of P/O Ambrose, 46 Squadron.*

8/JG54 Me109E-1 Wn.3470   Black 2+   The pilot was surprised by fighters and the engine stopped so he baled out. Aircraft fell at Finns Farm, Kingsnorth, Kent. Ff: Uffz Heinrich Elbers landed with wounds in his foot - PoW. *See report of F/Lt Hillcoat, 1 Squadron.*

1(J)/LG2   Me109E-1 Wn.3579, White 14+   Crash landing at Calais-Marck, 50%. Probably due to combat damage. Ff: Fhr Hans-Joachim Marseille safe,

Stab I/JG3 Me109E   Force landed at sea after combat with Hurricanes. Ff: Lt Detlev Rohwer rescued by Seenotdienst.

Other Luftwaffe Casualties

2 September 1940

Other Luftwaffe Casualties

5/JG3 Me109E-4 Wn.1443   Landed after combat at Marquise, 75% damage. Ff: safe.

6/JG3 Me109E-4 Wn.1469   Landed after combat 7 km WSW of Calais, 30% damage. Ff: safe.

8/JG51 Me109E-4 Wn.1632   Fell into the Channel after being damaged. Ff: Lt Braun rescued by Seenotdienst.

3/JG53 Me109E-4 Wn.1569   White 10+ Fell into the Channel after being damaged. Ff: Uffz Heinrich Rühl rescued by the Seenotdienst.

7/JG54 Me109E-4 Wn.1335   Crashed on landing following combat at Guines-Süd, 50% damage. Ff: safe.

3/JG77   Me109E-1 Wn.2695   Landed following combat near Wissant, 80% damage. Ff: safe.

3/406 Do18G-1 Wn.0868   K6+DL Fell into the North Sea. Shot down escorting an air-sea rescue boat and crashed 30 km north-west of Den Helder. Bo: Lt zur See Dietrich Logier and Ff: Fw Dietrich Christensen both killed, two crewmen rescued.

Night 2nd/3rd

The Luftwaffe sent 75 bombers on night operations, mainly to Coventry, but Newcastle and Filton were also on the target list. The bombs were so widely scattered that British Intelligence were unable to identify the intended targets.

TUESDAY 3 SEPTEMBER

729 RAF fighters fly 123 patrols. Luftwaffe - 90 bomber and 496 fighter sorties

Fine and warm in the south - rain or drizzle in the north.

COMBAT A 10.30 - 11.30 Richard Hillary 603 Sqn

COMBAT A
10.30 - 11.30 hrs... Attack on North Weald

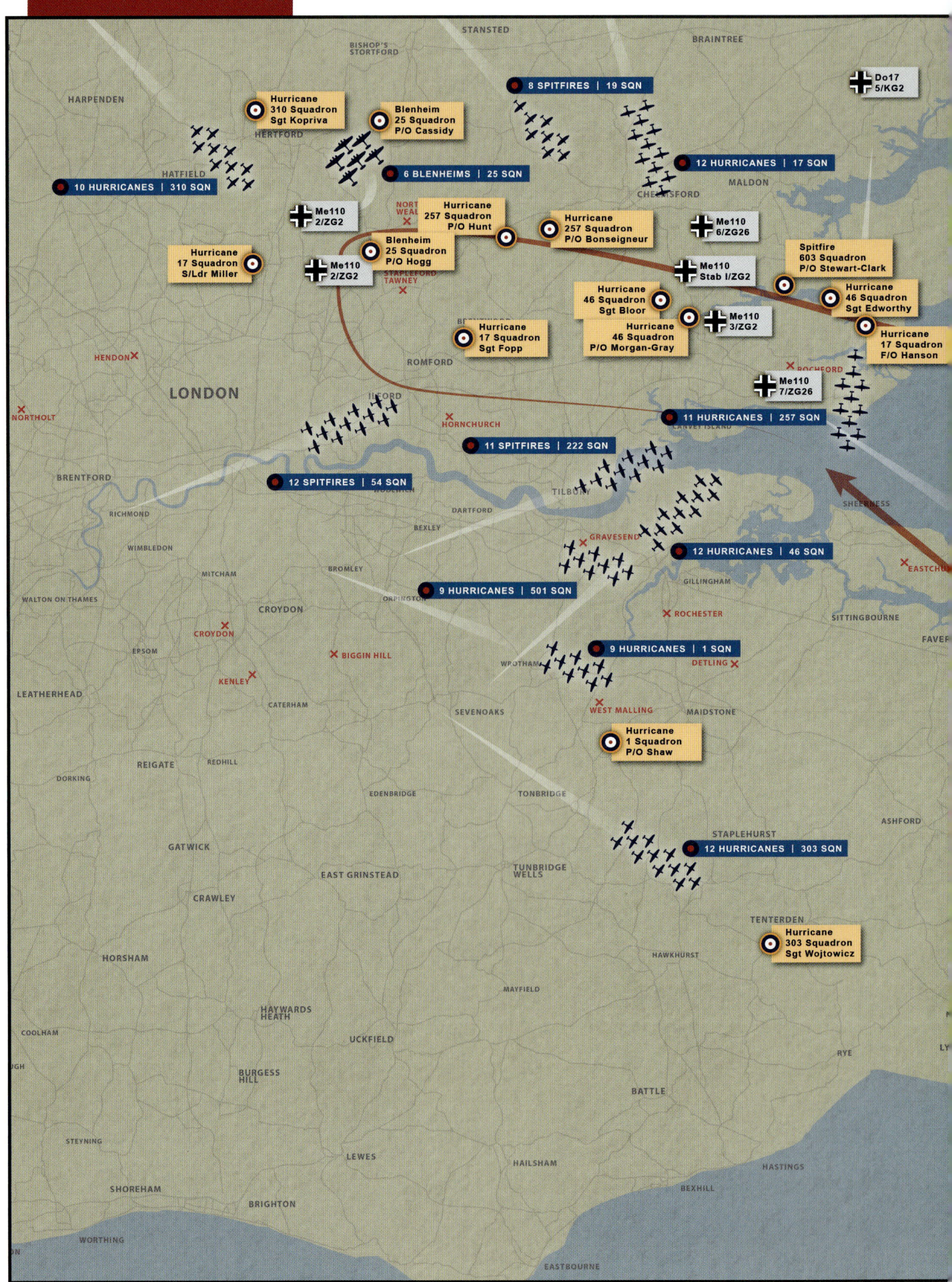

3 SEPTEMBER

Map labels:

- Do17 5/KG2
- 8 Spitfires | 19 SQN
- Hurricane 310 Squadron Sgt Kopriva
- Blenheim 25 Squadron P/O Cassidy
- 12 Hurricanes | 17 SQN
- 10 Hurricanes | 310 SQN
- 6 Blenheims | 25 SQN
- Me110 2/ZG2
- Hurricane 257 Squadron P/O Hunt
- Hurricane 257 Squadron P/O Bonseigneur
- Me110 6/ZG26
- Hurricane 17 Squadron S/Ldr Miller
- Blenheim 25 Squadron P/O Hogg
- Me110 2/ZG2
- Me110 Stab I/ZG2
- Spitfire 603 Squadron P/O Stewart-Clark
- Hurricane 46 Squadron Sgt Bloor
- Hurricane 46 Squadron Sgt Edworthy
- Hurricane 17 Squadron Sgt Fopp
- Hurricane 46 Squadron P/O Morgan-Gray
- Me110 3/ZG2
- Hurricane 17 Squadron F/O Hanson
- Me110 7/ZG26
- 11 Hurricanes | 257 SQN
- 11 Spitfires | 222 SQN
- 12 Spitfires | 54 SQN
- 12 Hurricanes | 46 SQN
- 9 Hurricanes | 501 SQN
- 9 Hurricanes | 1 SQN
- Hurricane 1 Squadron P/O Shaw
- 12 Hurricanes | 303 SQN
- Hurricane 303 Squadron Sgt Wojtowicz

78

Map Labels

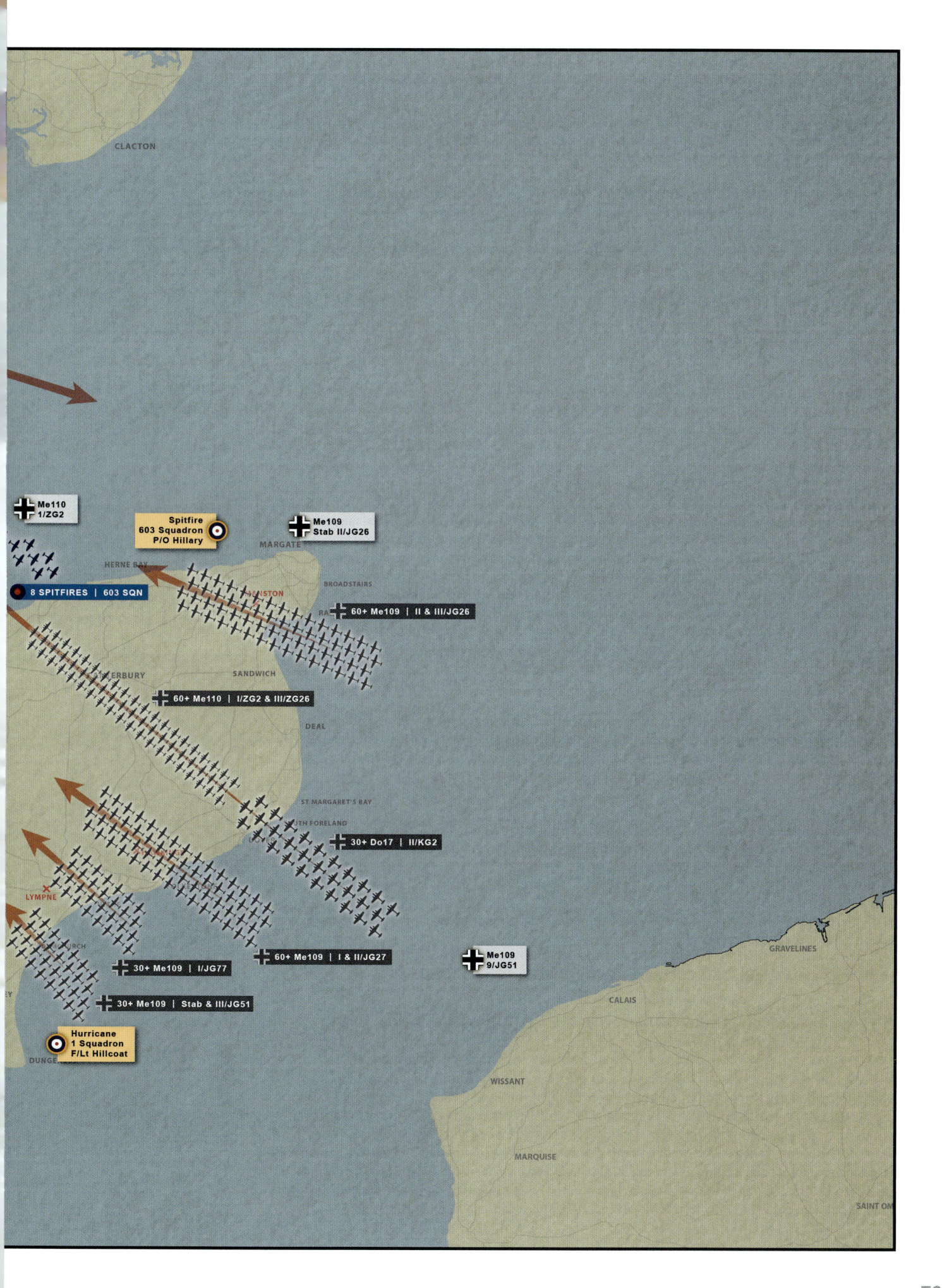

- CLACTON
- HERNE BAY
- MARGATE
- BROADSTAIRS
- CANTERBURY
- SANDWICH
- DEAL
- ST. MARGARET'S BAY
- SOUTH FORELAND
- LYMPNE
- DUNGENESS
- GRAVELINES
- CALAIS
- WISSANT
- MARQUISE
- SAINT OMER

Unit Markers

- ✠ Me110 | I/ZG2
- 🟡 Spitfire 603 Squadron P/O Hillary
- ✠ Me109 Stab II/JG26
- 🔴 8 SPITFIRES | 603 SQN
- ✠ 60+ Me109 | II & III/JG26
- ✠ 60+ Me110 | I/ZG2 & III/ZG26
- ✠ 30+ Do17 | II/KG2
- ✠ 30+ Me109 | I/JG77
- ✠ 60+ Me109 | I & II/JG27
- ✠ Me109 9/JG51
- ✠ 30+ Me109 | Stab & III/JG51
- 🟡 Hurricane 1 Squadron F/Lt Hillcoat

79

Luftwaffe Victory Claims

3 September 1940 - 10.30 - 11.30 hrs Combat A. Attack on North Weald

Luftwaffe Victory Claims		Combat A	10.30 11.30 hrs
St/JG26	Maj Adolf Galland	Hurricane	Chelmsford
St II/JG26	Hptm Erich Bode	Spitfire	Margate
St II/JG26	Hptm Erich Bode	Spitfire u/c	Margate
4/JG26	Fw Hermann Hoffmann	Spitfire	Hockley
4/JG26	Fw Wilhelm Roth	Hurricane	Wickford
St III/JG26	Oblt Josef Haiböck	Spitfire	Rochester
8/JG26	Fw Gerhard Grzymalla	Spitfire	10km south east of Southend
8/JG26	Uffz Arnold Küpper	Spitfire	10km south east of Southend
8/JG26	Lt Gustav Sprick	Spitfire	Rochester
8/JG26	Oblt Otto Meyer	Spitfire	Thames Estuary
9/JG26	Lt Johannes Naumann	Spitfire	Thames Estuary
2/JG27	Uffz Gerhard Fuchs	Hurricane	London
3/JG27	Oblt Gerhard Homuth	Hurricane	Burnham-on-Crouch
4/JG27	Oblt Gustav-Siegfried Rödel	Spitfire	in sea off Southend
4/JG27	Ofw Otto Schulz	Spitfire	Thames Estuary
4/JG27	Fw Karl-Heinz Bendert	Spitfire	Thames Estuary
4/JG27	Fw Karl-Heinz Bendert	Spitfire	Rochester
4/JG27	Oblt Gustav-Siegfried Rödel	Hurricane	Southend
St/JG51	Oblt Georg Claus	Spitfire	-
9/JG51	Uffz Kurt Koch	Spitfire	-
I/JG77	Unknown pilot	Spitfire	-
I/JG77	Unknown pilot	Spitfire	-
2/ZG1	Lt Eduard Tratt	Hurricane	north of London
8/ZG26	Oblt Sophus Baagoe	Spitfire	north of Southend
8/ZG26	Ofhr Alfred Wehmeyer	Spitfire	north of Southend
8/ZG26	Uffz Fritz Schupp	Spitfire	north of Southend
8/ZG26	Gefr Heinz Schumacher	Spitfire	north of Southend
8/ZG26	Oblt Sophus Baagoe	Spitfire	north of Southend
8/ZG26	Fw Walte Scherer	Spitfire	north of Southend
9/ZG26	Ofw Heinrich Hott	Spitfire	Chelmsford
9/ZG26	Ofhr Friedrich Lugger	Spitfire	south of Chelmsford
9/ZG26	Lt Kurt Sidow	Hurricane	Chelmsford
9/ZG26	Oblt Hubert Grisslich	Spitfire	Chelmsford
9/ZG26	Lt Kurt Sidow	Spitfire	Chelmsford
9/ZG26	Ofhr Friedrich Lugger	Spitfire	south of Chelmsford

Below: The Me110C, 3U+AS of Oblt Sophus Baagoe, the Staffelkapitän of 8/ZG26, who claimed a Spitfire during this combat.

Contemporary Accounts 54 Sqn

3 September 1940 - 10.30 - 11.30 hrs Combat A. Attack on North Weald

54 SQUADRON OPERATIONS RECORD BOOK

12 a/c of 54 Squadron left Hornchurch at 10.15 to patrol base and to intercept large enemy formations believed to be approaching base. They finally sighted a 50+ formation of bombers in large vic and a mass of Me110s. The S/Ldr of 54 gave orders for our a/c to attack just short of the aerodrome in order to upset the bombing attack. While 54 Squadron were preparing for this attack, e/a went to North Weald instead of Hornchurch. Control ordered our fighters to continue to protect Hornchurch, and it was only after North Weald had been bombed that they were ordered to the raid they had previously sighted. They attacked e/a in sections on their return flight to France. 12 Spitfires returned to base.

Enemy casualties claimed were:

S/Ldr Leathart	1 Me109 probable (smoke poured out)
P/O Gray	1 Me109 destroyed (landed on sea)
F/O McMullen	1 Me110 probable (gliding down with smoke from both engines)
P/O Baker and P/O Gray,	1 Me110 probable (e/a dived at ground with glycol coming from one engine).

Our casualties: Nil.

COMBAT REPORT:
P/O C F Gray — Green 1, B Flight, 54 Squadron

I observed a Me110 about 10,000 feet below me near the Southend Road. I half rolled and dived on its tail, opening fire at 150 yards and ceasing at 20 yards when I overshot. P/O Howes saw this Me110 diving at the ground afterwards with glycol coming from the engine.

Continuing eastwards over Shoeburyness, I observed a Me109 below me at 15,000 feet. I fired several good bursts and observed glycol as e/a dived down to sea level. I followed and chased him back nearly to the French coast firing the remainder of my rounds at very close range. More glycol poured out and e/a eventually hit the sea. I then returned as another Me109 appeared on the scene. Probably the destroyed e/a had called for assistance from the French coast.

COMBAT REPORT:
P/O S Baker — Green 2, B Flight, 54 Squadron

I was following P/O Gray when we saw an Me110 below us. He dived down on e/a, did a half roll on to its tail opening fire as he went. I followed him and did likewise and then dived away. P/O Howes later informed me that e/a dived at the ground with glycol coming from one engine. The combat was at 18,000 feet. Rear gunner of e/a opened fire on me, but the firing ceased after my attack.

COMBAT REPORT:
P/O B H Stapleton - 603 Squadron

When patrolling with 54 Squadron, I sighted a formation of 15 Do17s, accompanied by 20 Me110s. The enemy aircraft were flying in line astern and weaving about in S turns. As we had some 8,000 feet on this formation, the squadron went into line astern and attacked the Do17s. I fired at a Do17 in my first attack, with no visible effect. I climbed up again into the sun and attacked a Do17 which had one engine stopped. I attacked on starboard side, stopping the other engine with a deflection burst of 4 seconds.

Contemporary Accounts 17 Sqn

3 September 1940 - 10.30 - 11.30 hrs Combat A. Attack on North Weald

17 SQUADRON OPERATIONS RECORD BOOK

Weather mainly fair or fine; mainly moderate visibility but poor 02.00 hours to 10.00 hours. The squadron took off at 10.12 hours on patrol and sighted about 40 Do215s and Do17s with two large masses of fighters above them crossing the coast near the River Crouch. In the ensuing fight F/O Czernin destroyed one Me110 and probably another. Sgt Fopp went down with his a/c on fire, and baled out near Brentwood. He was badly burnt and is in Brentwood hospital; but is reported not on the danger list. S/Ldr Miller was attacked by a Me110 and force-landed in a field near North Weald. He was unhurt and re-joined the squadron later. F/O Hanson was missing, and has since been reported killed. He was seen to shoot down a Do17 into the River Crouch, after which his a/c crashed on Foulness Island. An observer reports that he tried to bale out at 100 feet. F/Lt Bayne, P/O Wissler and P/O Leary destroyed between them 1 Do215 and one Me110. P/O Leary also got one Me110 probable. F/O Bird-Wilson, P/O Rose and Sgt Sewell destroyed a Do215. One of the crew of each of the Do215 was seen to bale out. The squadron claimed a total of 2 Me110s and 2 Do215s destroyed and 2 Me110s probable; our own casualties being F/O Hanson killed and Sgt Fopp injured. P/O Wissler landed at Castle Camps with a damaged radiator. 8 a/c landed at Debden by 11.45 hours. At 14.50 hours the squadron again took off on patrol and landed at 15.45 hours. No further e/a were sighted.

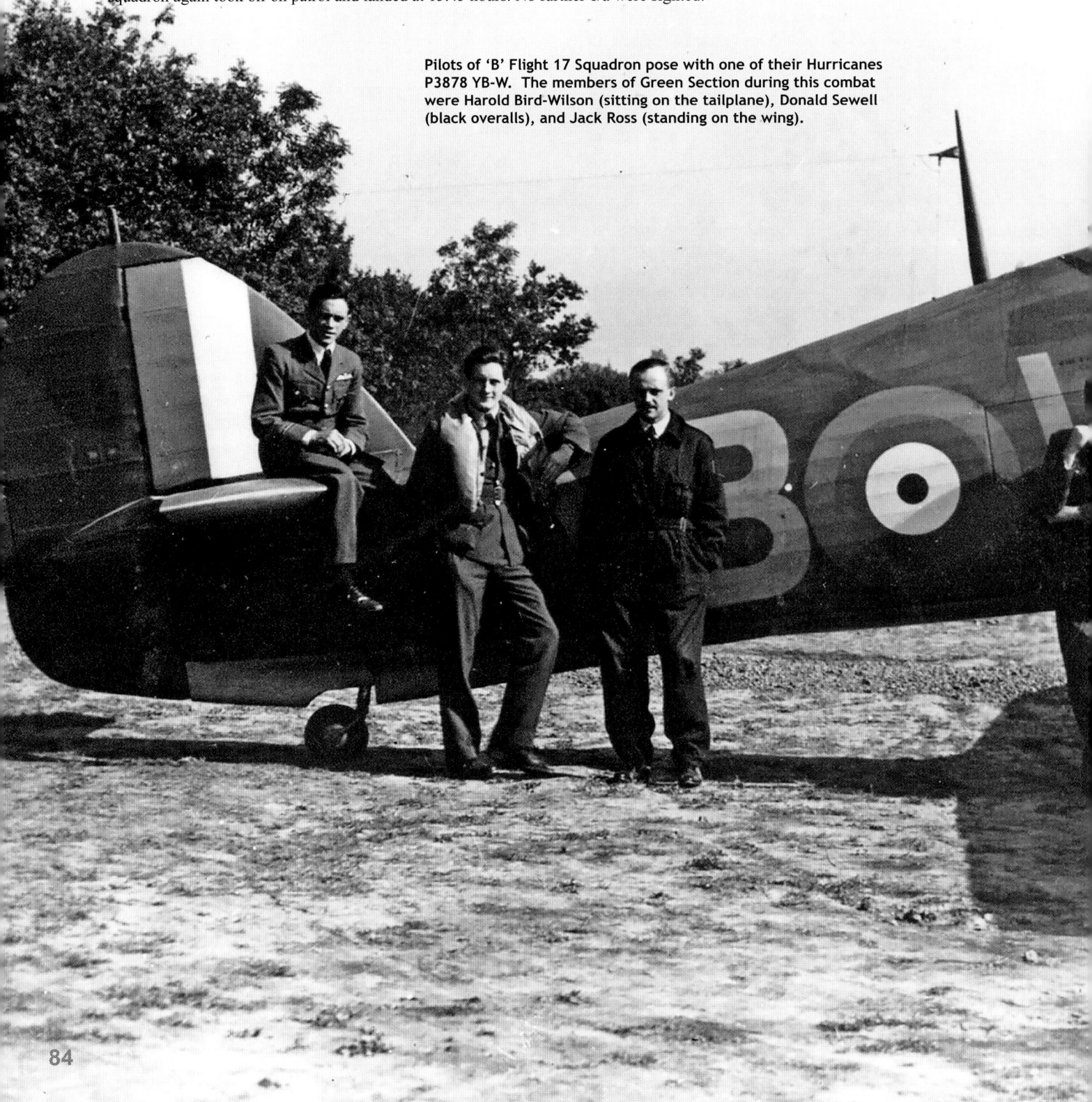

Pilots of 'B' Flight 17 Squadron pose with one of their Hurricanes P3878 YB-W. The members of Green Section during this combat were Harold Bird-Wilson (sitting on the tailplane), Donald Sewell (black overalls), and Jack Ross (standing on the wing).

Contemporary Accounts 17 Sqn

3 September 1940 - 10.30 - 11.30 hrs Combat A. Attack on North Weald

COMBAT REPORT:

F/O H Bird-Wilson, P/O J K Ross, Sgt D A Sewell - Green Section, B Flight, 17 Squadron

Whilst flying in squadron formation at 18,000 feet over the Thames Estuary, a formation of approximately 30 bombers, and approximately 100 fighters was sighted flying westwards at from 15 – 20,000 feet over the south of Colchester. Green Section, flying out of the sun, attacked a straggling Do215 which had broken away from the formation, and was heading northwards towards Ipswich. Two stern quarter attacks were made from the starboard side, Green 1 and Green 2 experiencing return cannon fire. On the second attack No.2 didn't fire, and as Green 3 broke away from his second attack the e/a was seen to go down in a vertical dive and one parachutist was seen to leave the machine. E/a crashed in the mud flats east of the reservoir, north of Colchester, and exploded. No bombs were dropped, Approximate length of burst for Green 1, 2 and 3 was 50 rounds. Visibility excellent. No cloud, slight ground haze.

Green 1 F/O Bird-Wilson   Green 2 P/O Ross   Green 3 Sgt Sewell

Contemporary Accounts 19 Sqn

3 September 1940 - 10.30 - 11.30 hrs Combat A. Attack on North Weald

19 SQUADRON INTELLIGENCE REPORT

Eight a/c of 19 Squadron were ordered to patrol between Duxford and Debden at 20,000 feet. They were operating in pairs, 2 a/c to each section. All a/c were fitted with two cannons except the Green leader's a/c which had eight machine guns. The weather was brilliantly fine, with excellent visibility. Whilst climbing towards the patrol line, the Squadron Commander, who was flying as Blue leader, was warned by the Sector Controller that e/a were approaching from the south-east; later he was told that they were over North Weald. On reaching 20,000 feet he saw explosions and clouds of smoke from North Weald; two isolated bursts of A.A. fire indicated the position of the e/a. These were heading east at 20,000 feet when sighted, and consisted of 50/60 bombers in three groups and close box formation, starting directly astern of the bombers and stretching upwards and backwards through about 5,000 feet were about 100 fighters, mainly Me110s all flying singly and turning, searching and weaving. Ahead of and above the whole formation was a single fighter.

Our squadron continued climbing on a course which would bring them up with this single a/c and planned to attack it first. On approach, however, other fighters left the main group and Blue Leader led the squadron into the attack on two of these which turned towards them. He fired at the left hand one which went past him and then turned to pursue it; having lost it he turned back and attacked another almost head on. He then discovered that his guns had jammed; he had fired only ten rounds from each.

Blue 2 attacked the right-hand a/c of the two and his starboard gun jammed. He was then attacked by two others but shook them off and fired at another until his port gun also stopped. He fired forty rounds from port and sixteen from starboard with gravity stoppages in each gun.

Green leader, with the eight-gun a/c attacked the leading fighter which dived towards the bombers for protection, so he turned and attacked two other fighters below him on his right. One of these dived away, and he opened fire on the other at about 250 yards range giving it a very long burst. During this attack the e/a employed violent evasive action ending in a vertical dive. Green leader followed it down towards the Thames but it eventually flattened out and flew towards Whitstable at a height of about 50 feet, still taking evasive action. On nearing Whitstable e/a turned towards the mouth of the Thames and flew straight and level. Green leader, who had been following now closed in again and fired the rest of his ammunition from 100 yards range. A piece of fabric came off the tail and the e/a dived into the water. Rounds fired 2,194. Green 2 stayed with Green leader and prepared to attack the same e/a; when he saw it destroyed he returned to base without firing.

Red leader saw the single fighter in front of the formation turn towards Blue leader during the latter's attack (this was presumably after Green leader had attacked it). He pursued it and, closing to 100 yards, blew his port engine out of the wing. As the e/a continued to fly and there was no return fire Red leader closed right in and fired the remaining rounds of his port gun, his starboard gun having jammed. The starboard engine of the e/a fell off and one occupant baled out. The a/c crashed south of Malden at the head of one of the creeks, possibly at Battlesbridge. Red leader fired 60 rounds from port and 6 from starboard in which there was a gravity stoppage.

Red Two fired at several a/c without result. He considers that he was using too much deflection.

Yellow leader carried out a quarter attack from above on an e/a on the port side of the formations. He experienced no return fire, and his attack ended as the e/a turned violently away and downwards. He could not follow it down as he had to take evasive action to avoid two Me110s which attacked him. He fired 33 rounds from the port drum with a gravity stoppage and 14 rounds from starboard with a deflector plate stoppage.

Yellow 2 attacked the same a/c as Yellow leader, but his guns jammed with gravity stoppages after firing only nine rounds from port and four from starboard. He saw the e/a go down with smoke issuing from it after Yellow leader's attack. Red leader had a cine camera gun and tried to switch it on but was unable to do so before being engaged.

R/T was satisfactory.
Reflector sights were used and were satisfactory.
There was return fire from some of the e/a but no hits were sustained by our fighters.

Blue 1 – S/Ldr Pinkham, A.F.C.	Blue 2 – P/O E Burgoyne
Green 1 – F/O L A Haines	Green 2 – P/O F A Vokes
Red 1 – F/Sgt G C Unwin	Red 2 – Sgt H A C Roden
Yellow 1 – Sub/Lt Blake	Yellow 2 – P/O W Cunningham

Contemporary Accounts 19 Sqn
3 September 1940 - 10.30 - 11.30 hrs Combat A. Attack on North Weald

COMBAT REPORT:
F/O L A Haines – Green 1, B Flight, 19 Squadron

I was on patrol with 19 Squadron leading Green Section at a height of 20,000 over base when we sighted black smoke coming from the direction of North Weald. On investigation we observed approximately 50 bombers in tight formation with numerous Me110s stepped up behind them as escort and went into attack the Me110s. I noticed one Me110 by itself in front and above the bombers but on attacking it, it dived towards the enemy bombers so I broke off the attack. I then noticed 2 Me110s on my right and just below so I immediately closed into a range of 250 yards and opened fire. The other Me110 dived away and I pressed home my attack. The enemy aircraft was camouflaged greyish above with black crosses on main planes and egg shell blue underneath. After a burst of approximately 5 seconds during which the enemy aircraft employed various evasive tactics, steep turns climbing and diving. I noticed some smoke coming from the port engine and the enemy aircraft dived vertically towards Thames. I followed it down and just when I thought it was going straight in it flattened out and headed towards Whitstable at about 50 feet off the water. Accordingly, I followed it occasionally closed in to approximately 100 yards whenever he was in a favourable position as in a climb. Two lines of tracer fire coming from rear turret were passing beneath me at commencement of attack.

When nearing Whitstable the enemy aircraft turned back and headed towards mouth of the Thames flying straight and level and with smoke still coming from port engine. I let it have the rest of my ammunition from 100 yards dead astern and I noticed a piece of fabric fly off and the enemy aircraft plunged into the sea.

Took off G.1 c10.15 hours, landed G.1 11.25 hours.

Below: Leonard Haines sitting on the nose of his 19 Squadron Spitfire in September 1940. Note the round gunsight, square ones only came into service after the Battle of Britain.

Contemporary Accounts 46 Sqn

3 September 1940 - 10.30 - 11.30 hrs Combat A. Attack on North Weald

46 SQUADRON INTELLIGENCE REPORT

At 09.55 hours on 3.9.40, 12 Hurricanes of 46 Squadron left Stapleford to patrol Rochford at 20,000 feet and intercept enemy raid 45. They encountered about 30 Dornier 215s and Ju88s, flying in six vics of 5 line astern at 15,000 feet, escorted by about 50 Me110s and Me109s. Enemy fighters were on the starboard side of, and astern of, enemy bombers and were stepped up to 2,000 feet. The formation was encountered about 6 miles west of Southend, flying west-north-west.

'A' Flight attacked the bombers from the beam, and 'B' Flight attacked the fighters but only a few of the bombers were detached, the main formation proceeding to bomb North Weald aerodrome.

Yellow 2 (P/O Lefevre) attacked a Ju88 out of the sun and set the cockpit on fire with a 2 seconds burst at 350/100 yards from dead ahead. He was himself attacked from behind by a Me109 and his aircraft hit in six places.

Blue 2 (Sub Lt Carpenter) destroyed a Do215 which may have been a Me110. He saw e/a forced-land in a field with its undercarriage up and one of the crew dragged another one out. This was 4/5 miles south of Maldon. He says e/a had dark upper surfaces and lower surfaces duck egg blue.

Blue 3 (Sgt Peacock) damaged a Do215 which gave out white smoke and dense black smoke from its port engine. He was unable to renew his attack as he was attacked from behind by Me109s.

Red 3 (Sgt d'Hamale) damaged a Me110 which gave out black smoke from its tail after he had attacked it from behind.

Red 1 (F/L Rabagliati) claims to have damaged two Junkers 88s, but only meagre details appear in his combat report.

Green 3 (Sgt Bloor) damaged a Do215, seeing pieces fall off its port engine cowling and a plume of black smoke. His own a/c was repeatedly hit and caught fire and he baled out and was slightly burnt.

Yellow 1 (Sgt Earp) damaged a Ju88 from above and behind and saw black smoke issuing from its port engine.

8 aircraft landed at Stapleford at 11.05 hours, and one landed later.

Our casualties: (a) Aircraft – 3 Cat.3
                 (b) Personnel – F/Sgt Edworthy missing.

COMBAT REPORT:
Sub/Lt J C Carpenter Blue 2, B Flight, 46 Squadron

At 10.20 hrs E/A sighted flying in large Vic formation at 200 mph WNW. E/A had dark upper surfaces, lower surface duck egg blue. Black crosses on the fuselage and wings. E/A 2,500 ft below broke up formation slightly as they observed us dive to attack. I made a beam attack on a Do215 which had broken away from the E/A formation. My first burst appeared to miss and I dived under his port wing to about 2,000 ft below. I then climbed and when almost level with the enemy I noticed an E/A single engined machine, probably a Me109, on my tail which I shook off by making a steep turn to the left and then noticed a twin engined E/A heading East. I came up to about 350 yds on his starboard quarter and gave him a short burst. He dived and I followed and gave him another short burst. He appeared to gain on me and pulled out at about 1,000 ft. I pulled out slightly above him, manoeuvred into position on his tail and gave him a long burst. He lost height and speed, I overshot him and turning saw the E/A land in a field with his under carriage up and go halfway through a hedge. I circled around, saw the crew get out and as one appeared to be dragged out presumed he was wounded. A farm hand approached the crew and then ran across a field to a farm house. When I went down again to investigate two members of the crew waved and as I saw that they offered no resistance to the farm hand I climbed up to identify the position as 4 or 5 miles south of Maldon, Essex and returned to base. This E/A was a twin engined, twin rudder A/C and was either a Do215 or a Me110. No fire was experienced from the E/A. Weather was fine, visibility 30-40 miles. Our attack from the South with sun behind and slightly to starboard.

Took off 09.55 hrs from Stapleford   Landed at Stapleford

Contemporary Accounts 46 Sqn
3 September 1940 - 10.30 - 11.30 hrs Combat A. Attack on North Weald

COMBAT REPORT:
Sgt R E de C d' Hamale – Red 3, A Flight, 46 Squadron

I was number 3 in leading section. When section leader gave order to attack bombers I dived on the starboard aircraft in the leading vic from beam and fired burst of 3 seconds. I didn't notice the result of it as I had to break away to avoid the fire of the rear turrets of the bombers. My aircraft was hit several times without suffering any damage. I then found myself within firing range of a Me110. I got on his tail and give it a burst of 5 seconds and saw black smoke coming out of its tail. I had to break away at 100 yards, when I noticed another Me110 on my own tail. Tracers whizzed past the cockpit, I managed to shake it off after a few minutes.

On my way home I noticed another Me110 at about 10,000 feet. I dived after it from beam and give it 3 bursts of 3 or 4 seconds. It went into a steep dive and I followed to the ground firing my machine guns until my ammunition were exhausted. I lost sight of the aircraft quite near to the ground near Southend. I didn't notice any damage.

Weather good but visibility poor in the sun owing to a thin mist.

COMBAT REPORT:
Sgt E Bloor – Green 3, B Flight, 46 Squadron

When E/A sighted, turned to starboard to approach out of sun with Green Section all going down to attack a formation of Do215s. I could see enemy fighters (Me110s) approaching on my starboard side. I had the Dornier in my sights at about 250 yds so gave a burst of three secs from beam position. I pulled hard around and gave it another burst into E/A's port quarter and saw small pieces fly off port engine cowling, eventually got a burst in from dead astern causing port engine to leave a plume of black smoke. I felt my aircraft repeatedly hit in fuselage when suddenly the instrument panel vanished through a hole in port side. The gravity tank was hit and flames came into the cockpit. I baled out immediately as a/c was not answering to the elevator controls and flames were obviously out of control. I was at 16,000 ft (approx) when I abandoned a/c and landed at Canewdon. Apprehended by Army personnel and taken after about two hours to Rochford.

Took off 09.55 hrs Stapleford

Abandoned a/c approx 10.30

46 Squadron pilots at Stapleford towards the end of the Battle.

Contemporary Accounts 222 Sqn

3 September 1940 - 10.30 - 11.30 hrs Combat A. Attack on North Weald

222 SQUADRON OPERATIONS RECORD BOOK

The squadron took off from Rochford to patrol Hornchurch at 20,000 feet. The squadron leader saw a circle formation of Me110s and made a full deflection attack, resulting in the enemy aircraft diving steeply out of control and confirmed by P/O Cutts following. Results: 1 Me110 probable.

Two 'A' Flight pilots engaged two enemy aircraft resulting in one Me110 falling with both engines on fire, and one Me109 crashing in the mouth of the Thames Estuary. Result: 1 Me109 destroyed. 1 Me110 destroyed.

Two pilots of 'B' Flight each claimed an Me110 and both these machines crashed on the land – one about 2 miles from Rochford and one near Reddington. Result: 2 Me110s destroyed.

One Sergeant pilot of 'A' Flight brought down a Do17 and an Me109 – this latter a chance combat while returning to base.

Another Sergeant pilot of 'A' Flight probably destroyed an Me110.

COMBAT REPORT:
Sgt E Scott – A Flight, 222 Squadron

I was flying at a height of 15,000 feet when I spotted a Do17 flying below at approximately 8,000 feet. I immediately dived and made a stern attack, giving enemy aircraft a good long burst. The enemy aircraft immediately dived to sea level with both engines on fire. I then closed in again and delivered another astern attack, giving two short bursts. The enemy aircraft dived steeply into the sea north of Manston. I saw a motor boat start away from the shore and go towards the wreckage, so I then made for home base.

COMBAT REPORT:
F/O B Van Mentz – B Flight, 222 Squadron

I was ordered on patrol with 222 Squadron. An interception was made and a fight ensued. I had several inconclusive engagements which I had to break off. On receiving instructions that enemy aircraft were proceeding south-east for North Weald, I proceeded to patrol Rochford at 20,000 feet. I saw a formation of Me110s crossing the Estuary in a south-easterly direction. I chose one of them and dived to attack. I gave him a sustained burst at the rear gunner and then the port engine. The enemy aircraft then dived steeply towards the river, finally turning towards Southend and landed about 2 miles inland, 3 miles east of Rochford.

COMBAT REPORT:
S/Ldr J H Hill - 222 Squadron

I saw about 15 Me110s in the usual circle formation above Hornchurch. I went in to attack one of them with a full deflection shot from his port side.

My first burst appeared to enter the rear of the aircraft, so I increased deflection and continued firing until my aircraft spun away. When I last saw the enemy aircraft it was diving very steeply towards the ground in a tight left-hand turn, evidently out of control.

P/O Cutts followed me in to attack the same aircraft and had to turn himself over on his back to give it a short burst as it dived steeply away.

Neither P/O Cutts nor myself saw any return fire.

Contemporary Accounts 222 Sqn

3 September 1940 - 10.30 - 11.30 hrs Combat A. Attack on North Weald

COMBAT REPORT:
Sgt S Baxter — A Flight, 222 Squadron

The squadron was patrolling at about 25,000 feet. We sighted about 30 Me110s going east over Rochford. The squadron formed line astern formation and we attacked.

At 12,000 feet I fired one burst at an Me110 without apparent effect, broke away, circled and attacked again from astern, giving about 5 seconds burst at 100 yards, closing to 50 yards. Both engines became enveloped in flames and smoke and the machine was blotted out due to smoke. I dived about 100 feet beneath, then came up and gave a burst about 50 yards from underneath. The enemy aircraft was last seen diving into the haze at about 3,000 feet with both engines still enveloped in smoke.

COMBAT REPORT:
P/O T A Vigors — A Flight, 222 Squadron

I dived with the squadron on 20 Me110s, opening fire at 250 yards. I gave one of the enemy aircraft a 4 seconds burst. Both engines caught on fire issuing forth black smoke and flames. The aircraft dived away from the formation.

I then found myself in the middle of the 110 formation. I gave four three-seconds bursts to 4 separate 110s at 50 yards range. I noticed that the engine of one of these caught fire.

COMBAT REPORT:
P/O J M V Carpenter - 222 Squadron

While on patrol we engaged approximately 30 Me110s. They adopted defensive circles about 5,000 feet below us. I picked out one Me110 that was not quite in the circle. I opened fire at a range of 300 yards from astern and fired all my ammunition in one long burst. I then broke away and saw him going down, two parachutes came out and the machine crashed somewhere around Reddington, north of Rochford aerodrome.

Editor's note: Should read Rettendon

COMBAT REPORT:
P/O J W Cutts — A Flight, 222 Squadron

I was climbing to regain the formation from about 4,000 feet when at about 16,000 feet I saw a number of Me109s below me heading east at about 12,000 feet. I was about to attack these aircraft when I noticed one Me109 straight ahead at a distance of about 50 yards.

As I noticed him he turned slightly to starboard and I gave him a short burst, after which his starboard wing broke away. I saw nothing further as I had been caught in his slipstream and was temporarily out of control.

I then dived down and returned to base.

This aircraft must have crashed in the mouth of the Estuary or just out to sea.

Contemporary Accounts 257 Sqn

3 September 1940 - 10.30 - 11.30 hrs Combat A. Attack on North Weald

257 SQUADRON INTELLIGENCE REPORT

Summary: 257 Squadron, while manoeuvring into position to intercept at 15,000 feet, a formation of about fifty enemy bombers which bombed North Weald at about 10.30 on 3.9.40., were attacked by isolated e/a's which swept down from a fleet of about 100 flying around at about 20,000 feet. One of the Me109s had a silvery camouflage on top and underneath.

11 Hurricanes, Blue, Red, Green and Yellow Sections, of 257 Squadron, left Martlesham Heath at 10.02 hours on 3.9.40 to patrol Chelmsford at 15,000 feet. One Hurricane, Yellow 3 (P/O Hunt) was delayed by a hitch at the start and took off at 10.07 hours.

Shortly before 10.30 hours, when the squadron was in the Chelmsford area at about 16,000 feet, flying south in vic formation, some of the pilots saw a formation of about 30 bombers about 2,000 feet above them to the south-east over the sea, flying west.

A large number of fighters were seen in very loose formation above the bombers. These formations were not seen by other members of squadron.

The squadron continued to fly on a southerly course and then orbited for some minutes while gaining height. After Blue 1, the squadron leader (S/Ldr Harkness), had given the tally-ho and had ordered the squadron into line astern, he flew forward at full throttle to intercept the bombers which were flying west, towards North Weald. He was apparently followed only by Blue 3 (Sgt Robinson). Blue 1, did a head-on attack on the bomber formation which appeared to be in four vics of about seven, with a large number of fighters some four thousand feet above. In his head-on attack, Blue 1 gave a 5 seconds burst, firing on two of the enemy bombers which had twin fins. The attack was followed up by Blue 3 (Sgt Robinson) who fired a short burst head-on at 300 yards, and then lost Blue 1, when he saw an Me110 outside the formation going towards it. He got on to the e/a's tail, opening at 300 yards and firing two burst of three seconds each, seeing tracer enter. At this time he was attacked from astern, so, having emptied his ammunition he made for base. Blue 1, after breaking away downwards to the right, pulled up to the left, but the bombers were well past him. After circling for about 10 minutes, with fighters above him, he called Kiwi and was ordered to return to base. No results were seen of Blue 1's and Blue 3's attacks.

Blue 2, (P/O Bon Seigneur) is believed to have been last seen by members of the squadron when slightly behind his section. According to eye witnesses at Ingatestone an a/c was seen to swoop down on him and his plane afterwards turned over and flew upside down before crashing near Margaretting. P/O Bon Seigneur fell among the trees at Ingatestone. According to the doctor, he received serious injuries in the air and there were traces of a bullet wound in the nape of the neck. His right arm was fractured. He is believed to have succeeded in extracting himself from the a/c, but not to have been able to open his parachute which apparently partly opened on hitting the trees.

Blue Section was split up from the other sections which were engaged by enemy fighters. At this time, Red 1 (F/L Beresford) saw about 20 Me109s above him. One of the e/a dived down near his section which dived after it to about 5,000 feet, but lost it in the haze. They then climbed as a section in line astern towards A.A. fire on the south-east.

Red 2 (P/O Gundry) states in his combat report that he observed a formation of 20 Me109s at 25,000 feet going west, and another formation of 20 Me109s passing above the section at 20,000 feet going south-east. 'While we were turning still in line astern as a section towards west and the north,' Red 2 continues, 'I heard gun fire and saw 1 Me109 attacking Red Leader from the sun above and behind on starboard side. While leader broke sharply to the left, I followed e/a round, and when he recovered, turned to the right, I got on his tail, giving three bursts at about 200 yards range, slight deflection.' The e/a was visibly damaged. An explosive cannon-burst shot off Red 2's port tail-plane and he spun down to about 3,000 feet before regaining control. Red 3 (Sgt Nutter) believes that he was the first of his section to be attacked. An Me109, which had a light silvery camouflage both on top and underneath, fired an explosive cannon shell into his starboard aileron, ripping it up. Splinters pierced his petrol tank, glycol return pipe and his legs. Red 3 then dived to 1,500 feet, set course for base and after a few minutes noticed a blazing Dornier east of Layer Breton reservoir. He followed and circled for 15 minutes above a parachutist two miles south of the reservoir, who came down in a branch of the River Colne and was picked up by a boat. He then returned to base.

Contemporary Accounts 257 Sqn

3 September 1940 - 10.30 - 11.30 hrs Combat A. Attack on North Weald

While the squadron was orbiting, Green Section dived at about the same time as Red Section. Green 1 (F/O Mitchell) saw a dog-fight proceeding between two Spitfires and e/a.

Green 3(Sgt Hulbert) went down to about 2,000 feet and saw a Spitfire circling in the opposite direction around a parachute which came down between rivers Blackwater and Crouch. He got split off from Green 1 and 2, who climbed up again, seeing a cloud of enemy bombers and fighters above them at varying heights, with a dog-fight, thought to be proceeding at about 18,000 feet. Green 1 (F/O Mitchell), followed by Green 2 (P/O Capon), circled up towards about 20 Me110s or Jaguars in rough line astern and closed in on them from 500 feet below. The Me's started to form a defensive circle flying left. Green 1 turned inside them flying right. As he was doing so an e/a came right out of the sun from above and made a head-on attack, firing above his head. Green 1 fired back for a split second. By this time, the circle of Me's had closed in. Green 2 did a steep turn to make a head-on attack when the leading Me which was 200 feet above him fired from about 350 yards, one bullet entering his port wing. Green 2 got into a violent spin from which he came out at about 10,000 feet, and having lost the e/a he returned to base.

Green 1 thought that Green 2 had been shot down, went into a steep turn and made a vertical dive, then went back to base.

Yellow 1 (P/O Cochrane) climbed up to 22,000 feet into sun when the squadron split up. After manoeuvring, he saw an Me110 at about 20,000 feet, chased it, firing a 2-second burst at about 300 yards, then saw tracer pass him from astern. He broke off and flew downwards after other stray e/a but returned without engaging them again.

Yellow 2 (Sgt Fraser), one of the pilots in the rear of the squadron who first saw the enemy formations approaching, was orbiting behind Yellow 1 before the tally-ho was given when he saw Yellow 3 overshoot him. Yellow 3 (P/O Hunt) had been delayed at the start and was catching up. Yellow 2 suddenly saw Yellow 3's cockpit on fire. He warned the squadron that they were being attacked from the rear, climbed in steep turns but saw no other e/a in the vicinity. He did, however, see fighters circling around at about 20,000 feet. At this time his section was about a mile behind the leading section. He came upon a straggler from a formation of about 20 Me Jaguars. The e/a saw him and tried to join his formation of 20. Sgt Fraser attacked his starboard side, firing continuously from astern until he saw pieces break off the e/a and the starboard engine on fire. Four of the main enemy formation of Me's then attacked him, and he was forced to break off the engagement. He stall-turned and went down to about 7,000 feet. After coming out of his dive, he saw the balloon barrage and Hurricanes returning to base. He was intercepted and recognised three times by Hurricanes at about 5,000 feet when flying back to base.

Yellow 3 (P/O Hunt) states that he was shot at from the rear, presumably from above. His aircraft caught fire, and he was able to bale out only after receiving severe burns. He was removed to Billericay Hospital. He is not yet out of danger but his condition is improving.

6 Hurricanes landed at Martlesham about 10.55 and four landed at Martlesham at 11.10 – 11.15 hours.

Our casualties:	P/O Bon Seigneur	...	killed
	P/O Hunt	...	seriously injured.

2 Hurricanes destroyed.
1 Hurricane damaged Cat.1.
1 Hurricane damaged Cat.2.

SUPPLEMENT TO INTELLIGENCE PATROL REPORT OF 257 SQUADRON 3.9.40.

P/O Gundry believes that when the port tail plane of his Hurricane was shot away by an Me109 on 3.9.40, at 10.30 hours, the following tactics were adopted. An Me109 which attacked leader of his section remained afterwards in P/O Gundry's sight without attempting evasive tactics, presumably because it was armour-plated. It did so to enable the Me109 astern of P/O Gundry to attack him with cannon. Although P/O Gundry visibly damaged the tail of the Me109 ahead, the pilot was certainly not hit.

Contemporary Accounts 310 Sqn

3 September 1940 - 10.30 - 11.30 hrs Combat A. Attack on North Weald

310 SQUADRON INTELLIGENCE REPORT

10 a/c 310 Squadron took off from Duxford at 09.26 hours to intercept enemy formation approaching North Weald from the south-east at 20,000 feet. F/Lt Jefferies was in command of 'B' Flight and a little ahead of 'A' Flight. 'B' Flight sighted a large formation of e/a Me110s and climbed above them and gave the order to attack from astern opening fire at close range. 'A' Flight led by F/Lt Sinclair D.F.C. (only four a/c) was protecting 'B' Flight at about 26,000 feet when he saw the bomber formation escorted by Me110s and ordered his section into line astern and manoeuvred up sun still keeping above 'B' Flight. He saw that there were no Me109s above the Me110s and he attacked from the sun and rear afterwards a dog fight ensued as the sky was black with e/a, the enemy bombers and fighters in close herring bone formation consisting of alternative lines of 5 Do215s and 3 Me110s this main formation being protected by further Me110s flying above it. Usual camouflage and markings. No hits sustained by fighters and no damage to a/c except that of Sgt Kopriva who baled out and is safe, no further information received about him. No cine camera guns carried. R/T was satisfactory, the pilots taking part and number of round fired are as follows:

F/Lt Jefferies	820 rounds	2 stoppages
F/Lt Sinclair D.F.C.	2400 rounds	nil
P/O Fechtner	400 rounds	no stoppage
F/O Maly	1440 rounds	nil
P/O Zimprich	160 rounds	nil
Sgt Furst	2100 rounds	1 stoppage
Sgt Kominek	400 rounds	nil
Sgt Vopalecky	800 rounds	nil
Sgt Koukal	1200 rounds	nil
Sgt Kopriva	No record.	

Below: Just like the Polish squadrons, the Czech 310 Squadron had a British Commanding Officer and Flight Commanders to help with integration into the RAF's way of doing things. Here we see 'A' Flight Commander Gordon Sinclair and C/O Douglas Blackwood, with some of the Czech pilots. L-R: F/L Jaroslav Maly, Sgt Rudolf Zima, Flight Commander Gordon Leonard Sinclair, P/O Vaclav Bergman, C/O George Douglas Morant Blackwood, P/O Vilem Goth, Sgt Bohumir Fürst, Sgt Raimund Puda, Sgt Josef Vopalecky, Sgt Jan Kaucky.

Contemporary Accounts 310 Sqn
3 September 1940 - 10.30 - 11.30 hrs Combat A. Attack on North Weald

COMBAT REPORT:
F/Lt G L Sinclair — Yellow 1, A Flight, 310 Squadron

I was Yellow Leader (4 a/c) of 310 Squadron on patrol at Hornchurch at 15,000 ft and then at North Weald at 20,000 ft, keeping my section at 26,000 ft to look out for fighters. We saw the enemy approaching N. Weald from the South East - a large mass of bombers escorted by many Me110s. I ordered my section into line astern and manoeuvred up-sun, still keeping above one or two sections and when I saw there were no Me109s I went into the attack, and went for a Me110, which burst into flames (confirmed by Sgt. Furst), and then attacked two of the E/A without apparent effect, and finally a Do215, by itself - which burst into flames just as I ran out of ammunition, after giving a long burst. I found that by climbing to about 22-23,000 ft after each attack I had a definite advantage, especially from the use of the sun, as the E/A remained at about 20,000 ft, after bombing N. Weald the E/A turned East. The Me110s did not appear to keep any formation, but just milled about behind the bombers. I received no return fire from Me110, but did from the Do215.

COMBAT REPORT:
Sgt F Koukal — B Flight, 310 Squadron

The attack was delivered on a formation of enemy bombers from the port from the sun from above. I carried out an attack as No.2 on Me110 from the port at the moment, when enemy aircraft turned to the left. I opened fire at him at 300 yards closing to 100 yards. The enemy aircraft crashed immediately after this long burst. F/Sgt Kominek who followed me as No.3 saw the enemy crash down. I also saw enemy aircraft Do215 crash down near North Weald aerodrome. The aircraft went into a left hand spin, having its port main plane cut off about one yard from the engine. At an altitude of about 10,000 feet I saw one of the crew bale out.

Took off from Duxford 09.40. Landed North Weald 11.25.

Below: The Me110 that Sgt Koukel had seen spinning down with a severed port outer wing was this one 3M+HL which had collided with another Me110.

Contemporary Accounts 310 Sqn

3 September 1940 - 10.30 - 11.30 hrs Combat A. Attack on North Weald

COMBAT REPORT:
P/O J M Maly – Yellow 4, A Flight, 310 Squadron

I was Yellow 4, and attacked from above an Me110. After getting in a long burst (100 rounds) e/a turned over and dived vertically, out of control, breaking off combat so I concluded it must be a total loss. I climbed to attack further Me110 and gave it a burst (20 rounds) without visible definite result. Both attacks from rear above at an angle of 20° to the right. Both e/a replied, but inaccurately. This lateral fire appears very limited in scope. Subsequently I could not regain favourable position to attack a further aircraft.

COMBAT REPORT:
Sgt B Furst – B Flight, 310 Squadron

The first attack was carried out by the leader of our section F/Lt Sinclair. I attacked the same enemy aircraft from the port. When I broke away I came on the rear of another Me110, which I attacked three times – twice from the port and once from the starboard. My third attack was delivered just at the moment when enemy aircraft made a sharp turn to the right. I fired on burst at range of 100 yards and the enemy aircraft crashed in flames south of Chelmsford. I could not continue the combat any more as I had no ammunition. I saw another enemy aircraft crash down in flames east of North Weald aerodrome. Took off 09.40. Landed at Duxford.

Below: Sergeant Bohumir Furst climbs out of his 310 Squadron NN coded Hurricane with the squadron mascot Rek there to greet him.

Contemporary Accounts 501 & 603 Sqns
3 September 1940 - 10.30 - 11.30 hrs Combat A. Attack on North Weald

501 SQUADRON INTELLIGENCE REPORT

Engagement of No.501 Squadron with part of a large enemy bomber and fighter force on 3.9.40 at 10.35 hours.

9 Hurricanes of No.501 Squadron left Gravesend to patrol Detling at 12,000 feet at 09.25 hours. They were vectored to the east Kent area and pursued aircraft to Herne Bay which turned out to be a Hurricane squadron (perhaps No.111). The squadron followed them back to Tunbridge Wells and became scattered in the process. Then Red Leader was forced to land at Detling owing to loss of air pressure. Red 2 and Red 3 heard over the R/T that North Weald was being bombed and flew in that direction. They sighted some 50 Dorniers bombing North Weald with an escort of some 150 Me109s and 110s at 15,000 feet to 20,000 feet. They were attacked by the Me110s which were dog-fighting with another Hurricane squadron. Red 2 was able to fire at a Dornier 17 before having to evade attacks by Me110s. Red 3 damaged an Me110.

All 9 Hurricanes had returned to Gravesend by 11.30 hours. E/a casualties 1 Me110 damaged. We had no losses.

603 SQUADRON INTELLIGENCE REPORT

09.15 – 10.30 hours, 3.9.40.

8 aircraft took off from Hornchurch. At 22,000 feet over Manston, they saw about 6 Do17s in vic at the same height and about 12 Me109s; above this formation was a further formation of 12 Me109s. The squadron attacked the fighters, which they considered to be inferior to any they had encountered before. The Me109s had no yellow noses. P/O Stapleton took off with 54 Squadron and when south of Harwich, dived on to a Do17 and shot it down.

Our casualties:
Pilots: P/O Stewart-Clark baled out – shot in leg in arm.
P/O Hillary baled out – slightly injured – burns.

COMBAT REPORT:
P/O J R Caister – A Flight, 603 Squadron

When on patrol with 603 Sqn, 12 or more Me109s dived on the squadron from above, a few miles east of Manston. Six Me109's broke away east from below and did not enter engagement. I attacked from astern, one Me109 and after a few seconds bursts it climbed steeply; closing up with a long burst I saw the e/a out of control. I had fired a few seconds burst at close range and broke off, and almost stalled. Turning away from the e/a I had attacked, I fired a few seconds burst at another Me109 almost dead ahead. This machine did not break off but passed me within a few yards distance. There appeared to be six streams of fire coming from the e/a. I did not observe any damage. I saw at least two and perhaps a third explosion on the water, either bombs or aircraft crashing. Turning round I looked for somebody of my squadron. I noticed an aircraft in my mirror, but I was too far away for it to start firing. Spiralling down in a steep dive I lost it, and being short of petrol I refuelled at Manston, taking off immediately and returned to base.

COMBAT REPORT:
P/O A P Pease – B Flight, 603 Squadron

I saw one Me109 over the sea about 5,000 feet below me. I could see no other aircraft above or below me, so I dived to make a beam attack. When I was still out of range, the enemy aircraft did a half-roll and dived vertically. It never pulled out, and crashed into the sea.

RAF Casualties

3 September 1940 - 10.30 - 11.30 hrs Combat A. Attack on North Weald

RAF Casualties	Combat A	10.30 11.30 hrs

1 Sqn Hurricane P3782   P/O R H Shaw – missing. Crashed at Parkhouse Farm, Chart Sutton, Kent. RAF salvors A V Nichols and Co were sent to the crash site on 29th September, but were informed that the aircraft had been recovered by the RAF the day before. It appears that only the wreckage remaining on the surface was cleared, leaving the pilot buried underground with the engine. Post-war the crash site became an unofficial memorial to an unknown RAF pilot, symbolising the men of the Battle of Britain. In 1972 a letter was discovered from A V Nichols addressed to the RAF's 49 MU, stating that Hurricane P3782 was the aircraft at Chart Sutton. From this it can be concluded that P/O Shaw's remains are still buried at the crash site; it is the wish of Robert Shaw's relatives that they are left undisturbed.

1 Sqn Hurricane P3044   F/Lt H B L Hillcoat – missing. Failed to return from squadron patrol.

Robert Henry Shaw (24)
Born: Astley Bridge, Bolton, Lancashire.
Joined the RAF in October 1937.
Joined 1 Squadron in March 1940.
Victory claims: - none.

Casualty File   Flight Lieutenant Hillcoat and Pilot Officer Shaw

The pilots concerned left Northolt at 10.03 hours on 3rd September, 1940, and were sent to intercept enemy raiders north of Dungeness. They encountered enemy fighters at a greater height than themselves.
The squadron was attacked, and it is presumed that the pilots were lost in the engagement which followed at approximately 10.50 hours.

Harry Bryan Lillie Hillcoat (26)
Born: London.
Joined the RAF in 1938.
Joined 1 Squadron on 10th May 1940.

Victory claims - 4:
4/6/40 He111 destroyed.
18/8/40 Do17 shared.
1/9/40 Me109 destroyed.
1/9/40 Me109 probable.

Just two days before, Hillcoat had spared the life of a German piot, allowing him to bale out to become a prisoner of war.

17 Sqn Hurricane R4224   S/Ldr A G Miller – safe. Shot down by Me110s and force-landed at Thornwood Common, North Weald.

17 Sqn Hurricane P3892 YB-I   P/O D H Wissler – safe. Landed at Castle Camps with a damaged radiator.

17 Sqn Hurricane P3673 YB-E   Sgt D Fopp – wounded. Shot down in flames. Crashed near Handleys Dairy Farm, Ingrave, Essex. Pilot baled out burned. Completely blinded he took 15 minutes to float to earth, landing at Creaseys Farm, Hutton. 20-year-old Desmond Fopp was admitted to Brentwood District Hospital with burns and remained in hospital for the next three months.

17 Sqn Hurricane P3539 YB-G   F/O D H W Hanson – killed. Shot down following destruction of Do17 and crashed on Brickhouse Farm, Foulness, Essex.

RAF Casualties continued
3 September 1940 - 10.30 - 11.30 hrs Combat A. Attack on North Weald

Extract from 1973 letter from Sergeant Fopp.

After getting a probable Do17 I was engaged by a couple of Me110s and ran out of ammunition. Whilst avoiding one of these the other dived away and came up underneath me and managed a burst of cannon fire in the belly of YB-E which really started a bad fire in the radiator which was below the cockpit and promptly set that on fire with me in it. I therefore left fairly hurriedly by parachute at about 17,000 ft, both burning, and I finished up in a wood about 2 miles from Brentwood.
My parachute was caught in the trees and I landed with my toes just touching the ground still smouldering - in fact I was still smouldering when I arrived at Brentwood District Hospital.
As soon as I landed I was set upon by the local farmer and had a bit of a job convincing him that I was British due to my burnt clothes. However, a few choice bits of language convinced him!

David Harry Wellsted Hanson (22)
Born: Hessle, Kingston-upon-Hull.
Joined the RAF in 1936.
Joined 17 Squadron in May 1940.

Victory claims - 5:
26/5/40 Do17 damaged.
3/6/40 Ju87 damaged.
14/6/40 Me109 probable.
12/7/40 Do17 shared.
3/9/40 Do17 destroyed.

Hurricane R.4174 F/O D W H Hanson
Missing on 3/9/40

17 Squadron was sent from Debden to patrol Colchester at 15,000 feet at approximately 10.00 hours. A large enemy bomber formation was sighted over the Thames Estuary, escorted by Me110s and Me109s. The squadron attacked the enemy formation. F/O Hanson's aircraft was seen by people on the ground to attack and shoot down a Do17 and then to crash in flames on Foulness Island. F/O Hanson attempted to bale out at 500 feet but his parachute did not open and he was killed.

Below: Desmond Fopp was shot down in this Hurricane P3673 YB-E. It was disliked by the pilots as it was missing the tips of the wooden propeller blades after an earlier accident. Fopp can be seen sitting on the wing, second left, David Hanson is believed to be the person sitting in shirt-sleeves nearest the shortened prop.

RAF Casualties continued

3 September 1940 - 10.30 - 11.30 hrs Combat A. Attack on North Weald

RAF Casualties	Combat A	10.30 11.30 hrs

25 Sqn Blenheim L1512   P/O D W Hogg – killed. Sgt E Powell (gunner) – baled out safe. Shot down over base by pilots of 46 Squadron who mistook it for a Ju88 and crashed at Greenstead Hall Farm, Greenstead Green, Essex.

25 Sqn Blenheim L8656   P/O E Cassidy, Sgt S Smith (gunner) – safe. Force-landed at Hatfield Heath, Essex, following attack by a 46 Squadron Hurricane over North Weald.

25 Sqn Blenheim L1409   S/Ldr W W Loxton – safe. Returned damaged by a 46 Squadron Hurricane.

Douglas William Hogg (23)
Born: Thornliebank, Glasgow.
Joined the RAF 1st February 1940.
Joined 25 Squadron 10th February 1940.

Victory claims – 1:
12/8/40 Ju88 shared.

Subject: Flying Accident – Blenheim L.1512

Sir,

Reference your letter dated 27th September 1940 regarding above, and this unit's Signal A.739 dated 3rd September 1940, I have the honour to report that the Blenheim aircraft L.1512 took off at approximately 10.45 hours on the 3rd September 1940 with Pilot Officer D W Hogg as pilot and Sgt Powell, 548940, as Air Gunner to patrol base since there was at that time a mass attack on the aerodrome.
2. The aircraft was serviceable at the time of take off and the magazines were full of ammunition.
3. The aircraft was shot down by a Hurricane machine, number unknown, and crashed at Ongar, Essex, at approximately 11.15 hours and was completely destroyed. The air gunner baled out and made a satisfactory landing without injury.
4. It was proved by both the air gunner and medical authority that P/O Hogg was shot and killed before the aircraft crashed.

25 SQUADRON OPERATIONS RECORD BOOK

'X' Raid Patrols were carried out by 3 Blenheim aircraft over base, when attacked by our own Hurricanes (unidentified) resulting in the loss of two Blenheims, P/O Hogg being killed, P/O Cassidy force landed at Hatfield. S/Ldr Loxton returned safely to base. Sgt Powell who was P/O Hogg's rear gunner was instructed to jump by the pilot before he died. Powell crawling to the front, the pilot dead over his controls, returning aft and jumped. The machine crashed about a mile away from North Weald.

Below: A 25 Squadron Blenheim prepares to taxi out for an operational sortie.

RAF Casualties continued

3 September 1940 - 10.30 - 11.30 hrs Combat A. Attack on North Weald

RAF Casualties	Combat A	10.30 11.30 hrs

46 Sqn Hurricane P3114   P/O P W Le Fevre – safe. Damaged by an Me109 over Rochford.

46 Sqn Hurricane P3063   P/O H Morgan-Gray – baled out wounded. Set alight attacking Do17s over Rochford and crashed at Apton Hall Farm, Canewdon, Essex. Admitted to St Margaret's Hospital, Epping.

46 Sqn Hurricane P3064   Sgt G H Edworthy – missing. Failed to return from the Essex coast. Crashed in Redward Creek, Burnham-on-Crouch, Essex. The aircraft was seen to fly out of control along the River Crouch, then dive into the mud. A boat was sent to the site and a large piece of the tail brought ashore, which was displayed to raise money for the 'Spitfire Fund' with a sign saying, 'Help Replace This One!'. It is assumed that Sgt Edworthy's body remains buried with the wreck to this day.

46 Sqn Hurricane P3094 PO-V   F/Sgt E E Williams – slightly wounded by shrapnel wounds in a leg. Landed at Debden with damage.

46 Sqn Hurricane P3024   Sgt E Bloor – wounded. Shot down over Canewdon and crashed into the seawall at Beckney Farm, South Fambridge, Essex. Pilot baled out with burns on face and believed to have landed at Scaldhurst Farm, Canewdon. Ernest Bloor's injuries prevented him re-joining his squadron.

Gerald Henry Edworthy (25)
```
Born: Newton Abbot, Devon.
Joined the RAF in 1930 and became an engine fitter.
Retrained as a pilot and flew with 263 Squadron in Norway in May 1940
Joined 46 Squadron in June 1940.

Victory claims – 1:
22/7/40 Do17 shared.
```

As no report was submitted to the Air Ministry regarding the loss of Sgt Edworthy, the Director of Personal Services wrote to the Commanding Officer of 46 Squadron in January 1941:

6231/40/P.4.Cas.   7th January, 1941.

The Officer Commanding,
No.46 Squadron, Royal Air Force,
Digby, Lincs.

Signal No.A.38 dated 4.9.40 – Loss of Hurricane P.3064

No reply appears to have been received to repeated applications to you for a written report regarding the above mentioned casualty, and this report should be forwarded forthwith.
It is pointed out that a brief written report 'giving a short account of the casualty and the nature of the duty on which the aircraft was engaged' is required in all cases of casualties due or presumed due to enemy action and reported under Message A, Note 3 of Appendix III to A.P.1301 (War Manual – Part II). In the case of aircraft lost by enemy action such reports are necessary for various reasons, e.g. in confirmation of the signal, enabling death to be registered and certified, or, if necessary, presumed. A record of the circumstances attending a casualty or last flight, moreover, is usually correspondence with next-of-kin.

(Sgd) J Earthy
for Director of Personal Services

The reply was brief:

25th January, 1941.

Loss of Hurricane P.3064 – Sgt Edworthy (564606)

Sir,

I have the honour to refer to your letter reference 6231/40/P.4.Cas. dated 7th January, 1941 and to reply as follows.
The above numbered aircraft was taken up on an operational flight by Sgt Edworthy on 3rd September, 1940, with the rest of the squadron, and this was the last ever seen of this pilot. As far as can be ascertained he was killed as the result of enemy action at approximately 10.30 hours on the above date.

RAF Casualties continued

3 September 1940 - 10.30 - 11.30 hrs Combat A. Attack on North Weald

RAF Casualties — Combat A — 10.30 11.30 hrs

257 Sqn Hurricane P3518 P/O C R Bon Seigneur – killed. Shot down over Ingatestone and crashed at Lodge Farm, Galleywood, Essex. Pilot baled out but fell dead at The Grove, Ingatestone, Essex.

Camille Robespierre Bon Seigneur (22)
Born: Gull Lake, Saskatchewan, Canada.
Joined the RAF in October 1939.
Joined 257 Squadron in May 1940.

Victory claims - 1:
19/7/40 Do17 shared.

Battle Casualties – P/O C R Bon Seigneur

Whilst patrolling Chelmsford at about 16,000 feet a formation of about 30 enemy bombers were sighted by the squadron at approximately 10.30 hours on September 3rd, 1940, escorted by a loose formation of fighters. Blue 1 (S/Ldr Harkness) ordered the formation into line astern and led the attack but was apparently followed only by Blue 3 (Sgt Robinson) who followed up the attack and emptied his ammunition and returned to base.

Blue 2 (P/O Bon Seigneur) is believed to have been last seen by members of the squadron when slightly behind his section. According to eye-witnesses at Ingatestone, an enemy e/a was seen to dive on him and his machine afterwards turned over and crashed near Margaretting. P/O Bon Seigneur apparently attempted to bale out but was unable to open his parachute and he fell among some trees at Ingatestone, and was killed.

His machine, Hurricane P.3518 was totally destroyed.

P/O Bon Seigneur's Canadian family wrote to the Air Ministry requesting further details of their son's death:

January 12th, 1941
My Dear Sirs,

P.354416-40-P.4. Casualties on September fourth you advised my wife of the loss of our son, Camille Robespierre Bon Seigneur – Pilot Officer. We have since been waiting in the hope you would advise us exactly what happened. We would like to know and believe we have the right to know just how he was killed, whether he is buried on land or in the sea. Was he burned or killed in the air?

Camille was our only child and you can well realize our feeling. We would feel much more satisfied to know all about it. Also we would like to know if he was successful in bringing down an enemy craft.

Please answer and give us whatever information you can, or if you cannot do it now – will we be able to get it at a later date.

His parents received the following reply dated 18th February 1941.

Madam,

I am directed to refer to your letter dated the 12th January, 1941, and to express regret that details of your son's death were not conveyed to you at an earlier date. According to the information at present available in this department your son Pilot Officer C R Bon Seigneur was the pilot of an aircraft which took off on patrol the 3rd September, 1940. About 10.30 a.m. enemy aircraft were encountered and during the ensuing combat it is stated by an eye witness that an enemy aircraft dived onto your son's machine which turned over and crashed near Margaretting, Essex. Your son was buried with service honours in Grave No.2 compartment 40 of the Saffron Walden Cemetery on 10th September, 1940.

I am to add that such further details as may be known to him will be conveyed to you by the Officer Commanding No.257 Squadron to whom a copy of your letter has been forwarded.

I am, Madam,
Your obedient Servant,

D P Ward
for Director of Personal Services

RAF Casualties continued
3 September 1940 - 10.30 - 11.30 hrs Combat A. Attack on North Weald

| RAF Casualties | Combat A | 10.30 11.30 hrs |

257 Sqn Hurricane L1585 P/O D W Hunt – wounded. Shot down and crashed near Brook Farm, Margaretting, Essex. Pilot baled out severely burned on face and limbs, admitted to Billericay Hospital. A nurse who saw him take 20 minutes to come down from a great height described him, 'burning like a candle wick hanging beneath his parachute'. He later became a plastic surgery 'Guinea Pig' at Queen Victoria Hospital, East Grinstead. David Hunt's injuries prevented him returning to operational flying.

257 Sqn Hurricane P3704 P/O K C Gundry – safe. Damaged when a cannon shell shot off the port tailplane

257 Sqn Hurricane P3705 DT-B Sgt R C Nutter – slightly wounded on right side and legs by shrapnel. Damaged over Chelmsford and returned to Martlesham Heath with a large hole in the starboard wing and fuel leak.

David Hunt wrote the following account which appeared in his wife, Esther Terry White's, book *A Pilot's Wife's Tale The Diary of a Camp Follower.* Published in 1942.

'On the morning of September 3, 1940, at 10.45, a Squadron scramble came through on the Ops phone. I had been allocated an old fabric-wing Hurricane of early war vintage, and had trouble in starting up. I took off five minutes afterwards, and shortly rejoined the squadron, which was circling D. at 20,000ft. We then sighted a large formation of German planes to port, heading for London, which we proceeded to intercept. Then a dazzling array of multi coloured light appeared on the starboard side of the cockpit, accompanied by explosive concussions. Immediately flame came through the instrument panel, filling the cockpit and burning my hands, legs and face. The reserve fuel tank had exploded, and I had neither gloves nor goggles, which I had pushed over my forehead to get a better view. I then tried to open the hood but found it had jammed. Using both hands on the one side, I managed at last to pull the hood open, undid my Sutton harness, grabbed my helmet off, and plunged out of the starboard side of the plane. I pulled my ripcord immediately, and assured myself at a glance that the parachute had opened. I then began to worry about being shot up on the way down. However nothing happened, so I started to survey the damage. My hands were all bloody, like I was feeling and they were covered with projecting tissue; that was the skin; and all that was left of my sleeve was a charred ribbon of rank. I was suspended in an ill-fitting parachute, and the air seemed so quiet after the roar of the plane that had terminated with the bang.

All I could hear now was the fluttering of the canopy, which reminded me of a yacht, and the fading drone and crackle of the battle going on above. I was worrying about the landing I should make, as I was swinging about like a mad pendulum in currents and gusts. When I was about 1,000 feet from the ground the sounds of shouting, dogs barking and a train whistle in the distance came floating up to me. After a 20 minutes' drop the ground suddenly began to come towards me quickly. Someone called "There he goes." There was a scrape, a swing and then a light bump. I had landed.

I lay as I was for a time, then sat up, and leant my arm downwards so that the ridiculous ribbon fell off my wrist, attached by a single thread. Then people started to arrive. Someone shouted "Keep back." I gave my name and asked them to ring the Aerodrome to say what had happened. Someone offered me brandy, and I said: "All I want is a nice drink of cool clear water"' which soon arrived and of which I drank a little. I was trying to explain to them how to undo my parachute harness. Someone else held up the parachute canopy to shade me from the sun, and someone said: "Don't move him. He may have bullet wounds."

The ambulance came and I parted with a reminder to them to ring my wife: the telephone number I did not know. And on the table where I had my first operation I breathed in the ether heartily and went out.'

Below: A section of 257 Sqn Hurricanes approaching to land.

RAF Casualties continued

3 September 1940 - 10.30 - 11.30 hrs Combat A. Attack on North Weald

RAF Casualties	Combat A	10.30 11.30 hrs

303 Sqn Hurricane R2688 RF-F   Sgt S Wojtowicz – slightly injured. Engine damaged by Me109 over the Channel. Landed at Woodchurch, Kent.

303 Sqn Hurricane V7246 RF-D   F/O Z Henneberg – safe. Damaged by Me109 over Dungeness.

310 Sqn Hurricane P8811 NN-F   Sgt J Kopriva – injured. Shot down by Me110s and wing tanks caught fire. Josef found he could not open his canopy and, as the fire took hold, he was thrown clear. Aircraft crashed at Rookes Farm, Hunsdon, Hertfordshire. Josef Kopriva suffered burns to his hands and face that prevented him flying operationally until 26th October.

603 Sqn Spitfire X4277 XT-M   P/O R H Hillary – wounded. Shot down in flames off Margate. Pilot baled out burnt on hands, legs and face, rescued by Margate life-boat. Admitted to Margate General Hospital. 21-year-old Australian Richard Hillary became a plastic surgery 'Guinea Pig' at Queen Victoria Hospital, East Grinstead, until the end of 1941.

603 Sqn Spitfire X4185 XT-Z   P/O D Stewart-Clark – wounded. Abandoned over Burnham-on-Crouch, Essex, after being damaged off Margate. Aircraft fell ½ mile north of Creeksea Church. Pilot admitted to Chelmsford Hospital with injuries to his left arm and foot.

Accident to Hurricane R2688 – FB

Herewith report in amplification of Signal A16 concerning the crash of Hurricane R2688 piloted by Sgt Wojtowicz.
This pilot was ordered on an offensive patrol and engaged an Me109 near Dungeness which he pursued down and out over the Channel, firing three bursts into it from about 100 yards range. Immediately after the third burst a lot of hot oil came back into the cockpit of the Hurricane and covered the goggles of the pilot thus preventing him seeing. When he was again able to see the aeroplane was in a steep spiral dive and although he attempted to jump out, as the engine was on fire, he was unable to do so.
Eventually he succeeded in regaining control and at the same time the fire went out and he turned and glided towards the English coast eventually landing with his undercarriage down in a field near Woodchurch, Kent. Unfortunately the field sloped downhill and had an orchard at the bottom of it and when the pilot applied his brakes he found they would not work so he ran into the trees, causing further damage to the aeroplane.
During the glide towards the coast the pilot opened the throttle but got no pull from the airscrew so he switched off. On examination after landing it was found that the airscrew and part of the engine cowling had been shot off. A cannon shell was found lying under the nose of the aeroplane and appeared to have come out of the engine bay, it is possible that the Hurricane was attacked from behind by a second Me109 whilst attacking the first Me109.

Accident to Spitifre X.4277.
Signal A.334 d/d.3.9.40
P/O R H Hillary (76477).

Sir,

I have the honour to report that on 3rd September, 1940, Pilot Officer R H Hillary was the pilot of Spitfire X.4277 when eight aircraft of No.603 Squadron took off from Hornchurch on defensive patrol.
At 22,000 feet over Manston a number of enemy bombers and escorting fighters were seen and there was a dog fight with the fighters.
Pilot Officer Hillary shot one down but in following it down his own aircraft was hit and started to burn. He experienced considerable difficulty in getting out and in consequence was severely burnt. He spent two hours in the Thames Estuary and was picked up by a lifeboat from Margate where he was taken to hospital.

Luftwaffe Casualties

3 September 1940 - 10.30 - 11.30 hrs Combat A. Attack on North Weald

| Luftwaffe Casualties | Combat A | 10.30 11.30 hrs |

Stab II/JG26 Me109E-4 Wn.0823   Black < + - Failed to return from Margate. Ff: Lt Eckhardt Roch - missing.

3/JG27 Me109E-1 Wn.6237   Ditched 23 km north east of Dunkirk. Ff: Fw Wilhelm Harting - wounded.

4/JG27 Me109E-1 Wn.6336   White 9+ - Collided on take-off from Fiennes with Black 15+ which was landing - 95% damage. Ff: Uffz Wilhelm Morgenstern injured.

5/JG27 Me109E-1 Wn.2686 Black 15+ - Collided when landing at Fiennes with White 9+, 70% damage. Ff: Emmerich Fluder wounded.

9/JG51 Me109E-1 Wn.6290   Fell into the Channel. Ff Gefr Robert Kuhn baled out and rescued wounded.

4/JG53 Me109E-4 Wn.1244 White 5+ - Landed at Sempy, 9 km north east of Montreuil-sur-Mer - 55% damaged. Ff: safe.

5/KG2 Do17Z-2   Wn.3450   U5+AN The whole of II/KG2, escorted by a mixed force of about twenty Me109s and Me110s were to attack North Weald aerodrome. The bombers were flying in Gruppenkeil formation (Gruppe, Staffel Vic, Ketten Vic astern) when they were intercepted by fighters and the pilot scuttled the bombs in an effort to escape. Aircraft fell near Pyefleet Creek, Lodge Farm, Langenhoe, Essex, was completely destroyed and buried twenty feet underground. Ff: Lt Heinz Schildt, Bf: Gefr Paul Niegisch and Bm: Uffz Emil Swientek all missing. Bo: Fw Martin Kriegel - PoW.
See report of Green Section 17 Squadron and Red 3 (Sgt Nutter) 257s Squadron Intelligence Report, who circled one of the crew who came down in the River Colne.

Stab I/ZG2 Me110C-4 Wn.3120   3M+CB While flying at 19,000 feet attacked by six 'Spitfires' when the crew went to help another Me110 which was in trouble. . Both crew baled out and aircraft fell on the lawn of Edwins Hall, Woodham Ferrers, Essex. Ff: Oblt Reinhold Messner and Bf: Ogefr Alois Santoni - PoWs.
See report of P/O Carpenter, 222 Squadron.

2/ZG2 Me110C-4 Wn.2146   3M+BK Engaged at 13,000 feet by a Hurricane and one of the engines caught fire, so the crew baled out. Aircraft fell in the sea off Herne Bay, Kent. Ff: Oblt Siegfried Gottschalt PoW with a broken ankle. Bf: Uffz Max Hoffmann PoW. *See report of Sgt Scott, 222 Squadron.*

Right: Me110 pilot Lt. Reinhold Messner (left) smiles as Lt. Gerhard Granz pokes fun at his EKI. Messner was shot down on 3rd September 1940; Granz followed him into captivity four days later.

Luftwaffe Casualties continued

3 September 1940 - 10.30 - 11.30 hrs Combat A. Attack on North Weald

| Luftwaffe Casualties | Combat A | 10.30 11.30 hrs |

2/ZG2 Me110C-4 Wn.2065   3M+EK Following a mid-air collision with Me110 3M+HL the crew baled out, but neither of their parachutes opened properly; one appeared to have opened but must have got caught in the aircraft. The aircraft crashed at Hobbs Cross, Epping, Essex, and exploded fifty minutes later. Ff: Fw Kurt Wagenbreth and Bf: Uffz Aribert Schubarth both killed.

2/ZG2 Me110C-4 Wn.2133   3M+HL Flying above the bombers at about 24,000 feet, this crew collided with Me110 3M+EK. The collision smashed the port wing-tip and rudder and the aircraft fell at Rye Hill, Thornwood, Epping, Essex. 2nd Staffel crew flying a 3rd Staffel aircraft. Ff: Oblt Kurt Müller - baled out PoW. Bf: Uffz Johannes Korn – killed. *See reports of 310 Squadron.*

Left and Below: The two Me110s that collided over Epping during this combat. Left is the remains of 3M+HL and below is 3M+EK photographed a few days before the collision.

Luftwaffe Casualties continued
3 September 1940 - 10.30 - 11.30 hrs Combat A. Attack on North Weald

| Luftwaffe Casualties | Combat A | 10.30 11.30 hrs |

3/ZG2 Me110C-4 Wn.3113 3M+EL Attacked by three 'Spitfires' from above. Both crew baled out and the aircraft fell at Pudsey Hall Farm, Canewdon, Essex. Ff: Ofw Gerhard Winkler – PoW slightly wounded, Bf: Gefr Oscar Weiler PoW. *See reports of 17 Squadron and Red 1, F/Sgt Unwin in the 19 Squadron intelligence Report.*

3/ZG26 Me110C-4 Wn. 3294 U8+KL Attacked over the Channel and the wireless operator baled out and his body washed ashore at Southend. Pilot forced landed at Fontend, France. Bf: Uffz Horst Klatt - killed. Ff: - safe.

Above: Me110 U8+KL which force landed at Fortend in France after this combat, without its rear gunner who had baled out.

6/ZG26 Me110D Wn.3310 3U+EP Both engines were hit and stopped by fighters and the pilot made a good landing near the Maldon to Latchingdon Road, Mundon, Essex. Ff: Lt Walther Manhart – Pow. Bf: Uffz Werner Drews - PoW severely wounded.
See report Sub Lt Carpenter, 46 Squadron.

6/ZG26 Me110C-4 Damaged by fighters and crashed on return. Ff: safe. Bf: Uffz Rudolf Löhr wounded.

7/ZG26 Me110C-2 Wn.3225 3U+KR Shot down from 21,000 feet and fell near North Shoebury House, Essex. The pilot was wounded in the head and shoulder from a rear attack. Ff: Fw Hans Grau PoW wounded. Bf: Uffz Günther Uecker seriously wounded, died 4th September.
See report of F/O van Mentz, 222 Squadron.

9/ZG26 Me110C-4 Wn.3578 3U+GT Crashed on landing at Wissant - 80% damaged. Ff: Ofw Heinrich Hott and Bs both safe.

Right: The Me110 force suffered heavy casualties in this combat, this is 3U+GT which limped back across the Channel before force landing at Wissant.

Other Incidents

3 September 1940 - 14.00 - 16.00 hrs

At 14.00 hours an attack of 100+ aircraft crossed the stretch of coast between Dungeness and North Foreland in small numbers and made in the general direction of the Thames Estuary. No less that twelve squadrons were scrambled, but only two sighted the enemy and only two pilots made a claim. Although a few bombs were scattered the RAF believed that the sole purpose of the raids were to keep Fighter Command in the air for as long as possible.
No RAF or Luftwaffe lost due to combat.

Luftwaffe Intelligence Summary
15.15 hrs. Maidstone Airfield. 44 SC 50 bombs. Large hangar seen burning.

RAF Victory Claims			14.00 - 16.00 hrs	
303 Sqn	Sgt J Frantisek	He113 destroyed	Mid-Channel	15.40 hrs
222 Sqn	Sgt E Scott	Me109 destroyed	off Folkestone	16.00 hrs

Luftwaffe Victory Claims	14.00 - 16.00 hrs

No victory claims filed.

303 SQUADRON INTELLIGENCE REPORT

Combat at 15.40 hours mid-Channel from Dover. 9 Hurricanes up 14.15 hours, down 16.10.

Enemy casualties.   1 He 113 destroyed.
Our casualties.   Nil.

The squadron after various Group orders was vectored to patrol between Maidstone and Dover. They met numbers of friendly fighters, and saw no enemy formation. Sgt Frantisek Green 2, rear guard, descended south-eastwards from 22,000 feet to investigate aircraft at 8,000 feet above cloud. They were Spitfires. He descended below cloud and saw a solitary He 113 immediately below him over the sea. He dived out of the sun and closed to 100 yards firing a two seconds burst into the cockpit. E/A dived slowly and disappeared into the sea mid-Channel from Dover.

The rest of the squadron had meanwhile been ordered to return home and Sgt Frantisek returned independently, arriving a few minutes after them.

Right: Josef Frantisek a Czech pilot serving with 303 (Polish) Squadron quickly became a 'lone wolf', often detaching from the squadron and finding his own enemy aircraft. This combat is a perfect example of his approach which the squadron eventually tolerated because of his apparent success.

Other Incidents
3 September 1940 - 14.00 - 16.00 hrs

222 SQUADRON OPERATIONS RECORD BOOK

Sgt Scott shot down a Me109 while flying a u/s machine from Rochford to Hornchurch. He intercepted the e/a as it was about to deliver an attack on an aircraft of the squadron which had first taken off. He pursued it to the coast, the e/a eventually diving into the sea off Folkestone.

COMBAT REPORT:
Sgt E Scott — A Flight, 222 Squadron

I was ordered to take a U/S machine to home base for repair. On taking off, I noticed that my squadron was about to take off also. I climbed above the clouds and waited for my squadron. I sighted them in the distance, so I went full out and eventually caught them up. I was just in time to see one Me109 about to make an attack on one of our aircraft, the height of which was approximately 8,000 feet. I immediately made a steep-turn and got on his tail, giving chase. He climbed to about 15,000 feet. I climbed with engine full out and kept 500 feet below him, but could not get any nearer than 600 yards. I decided to try a long shot. This appeared to have effect because the machine dived very steeply towards sea level. I followed him down and was able to close in from 600 yards to 10 yards and expended all my ammunition. I found I had gathered too much speed and overshot him, so I did a steep turn to port and was able to see the Me109 hit the water with a big splash. I did not stay to make any further investigation because I saw two or three black dots coming towards me which I imagined to be enemy aircraft, so I went full out and hedge-hopped to Maidstone, where I tried to get refuelled.

Below: Sgt Ernest Scott stands next to a very war-weary 222 Squadron Spitfire.

Other RAF Casualties

3 September 1940

Other RAF Casualties	3rd September

07.00 hrs
253 Sqn Hurricane P3610 P/O L C Murch – safe. Crashed into a wood at Nonnington during squadron sortie.

07.30 hrs
222 Sqn Spitfire L1010 Sgt R B Johnson – slightly injured. Abandoned over Burnham having developed a glycol leak during routine patrol. Crashed at Lower Raypits, Canewdon, Essex.

14.45 hrs
72 Sqn Spitfire X4262 Crashed at Pattenden Lane, Marden, Kent. One of the most mysterious losses of the Battle. X4262 was proven to have crashed at Pattenden Lane when it was recovered in the 1970s. Maidstone ARP Centre logged the crash and reported that the pilot had baled out safely, but 72 Squadron does not record any activity for 3rd September and there is no record of who was flying the aircraft, or why he baled out. The name F/O T A F Elsdon has been linked to this incident in post-war research.

15.55 hrs
249 Sqn Hurricane V6635 Sgt P A Rowell – safe. Damaged by AA fire during a patrol over Dover and crashed on landing. The pilot was unaware that he had been hit until the Hurricane caught fire just before he landed at North Weald, he was slightly concussed in the heavy landing.

Night 3rd/4th

The Luftwaffe sent 90 bombers on night operations, to Rochester, Liverpool and Bristol.

RAF Victory Claim			21.30 hrs
87 Sqn	P/O R P Beamont	E/A damaged	Wells

87 SQUADRON INTELLIGENCE REPORT

P/O Beamont of 'B' Flight 87 Squadron when patrolling Milk 'A', south-east of Bristol at 10,000 feet sighted an e/a illuminated by searchlights; shells were bursting round it. E/a was diving from 7,000 to avoid lights and firing down one of the beams. Just before e/a left beams P/O Beamont fired one burst of 5 seconds from 350 yards, saw his incendiary bullets hit e/a which dived so steeply that it looked as though it would crash but nothing further could be seen. Off from Bibury 21.10 hours, landed Bibury 22.45 hours. No return fire from e/a.

Left: Roland Beamont in the cockpit of an 87 Squadron Hurricane painted with unusual victory markings.

The problem with 616 Squadron

Keith Park continued to express his displeasure with Leigh-Mallory and the squadrons he had been provided with as reinforcements by 12 Group.

Message from Headquarters 11 Group
to
Fighter Command

Sector Commander Kenley reports 616 Squadron have made second application to return to their station in 12 Group which he strongly recommends because of their low fighting efficiency. During its two weeks in the south the squadron has suffered heavy casualties for small results and it is requested that they be replaced by a squadron from 10 or 13 Group if 12 Group is unable to spare an experienced squadron.

Although Park regarded 616 Squadron as inexperienced, many of its pilots had been with it from pre-war days and eleven had flown Spitfires over the Dunkirk beaches. The commanding officer, 28-year-old Marcus Robinson, had joined 602 Squadron in 1933, became 'A' Flight Commander in 1938, attacked Ju88s over the Firth of Forth in October 1939 and shared in the shooting down of an He111 in January 1940. He took command of 616 Squadron on 1st May 1940, damaged an Me109 over Dunkirk, claimed a probable Ju88 on 6th August and another on 15th August.

Presumably blamed for the squadron's 'low fighting efficiency' he was relieved of his command on 3rd September to become an instructor at 1 Flying Training School, Leuchars and never returned to operational flying.

Below: Despite the squadron being withdrawn from the frontline on 3 September, it was back in action before the end of the month as the Luftwaffe turned its attention towards London and within range of 12 Group. This photo shows 616 Squadron Spitfires operating from Duxford or Fowlmere on 26 September 1940.

616 Squadron in 11 Group: 20 August - 3 September

616 Sqn Pilots	Arrived	20-Aug	21-Aug	22-Aug	23-Aug	24-Aug	25-Aug	26-Aug	27-Aug	28-Aug	29-Aug	30-Aug	31-Aug	1-Sep	2-Sep	3-Sep
P/O H S L Dundas	Oct-39															
Sgt P T Wareing	Jun-40			SD wounded												
Sgt T E Westmoreland	Jul-40			Claim												
F/O G E Moberly	Nov-38															
F/O R Marples	Dec-39							SD killed								
F/Lt E F St Aubyn	Aug-40						Claim	SD killed								
Sgt M Ridley	Early 40							SD wounded								
F/O W L B Walker	Jun-40							SD wounded								
Sgt P Copeland	Early 40							SD wounded								
F/O J S Bell	Aug-39						Claim	SD safe					SD killed			
F/O J M Hewson ex Fairey Battle pilot	21 Aug 40		from 142 Sqn				SD POW									
F/Lt D E Gilham	Sep-39										Claim	4 Claims	Claim	3 Claims	Posted to 15 FTS	to Coltishall
P/O K Holden	Jan-40							Returned from nav course						2 Claims	Claim SD safe	to Coltishall
P/O D S Smith	Sep-39											Claim		Claim	Claim	to Coltishall
Sgt J Hopewell	Jul-40											Claim Crashed		Claim	Claim	to Coltishall
P/O L H Casson	Jul-40											Claim		Claim		to Coltishall
S/Ldr M Robinson	May-40													Claim		Relieved of command
P/O J Brewster	Jul-40													3 Claims		to Coltishall
F/Sgt F P Burnard	Jun-40													2 Claims		to Coltishall
F/Lt R O Hellyer	Nov-38															to Coltishall
P/O T B Murray	Apr-40															to Coltishall
Patrols flown		1	2	1	1	4	1	1	0	4	2	4	3	2	4	1

SD = Shot Down

112